From Stethoscope to Gavel

From Stethoscope to Gavel

Of becoming a doctor, lawyer and judge.

Dr Harry Rein JD MD

Physician - Lawyer - Judge

ISBN-13: 9780692521076
ISBN-10: 0692521070
Library of Congress Control Number: 2015914170
Dr. Harry Rein, Longwood, FL
Edited by Charlene Smith, Transformative Writing, Boston
www.charlenesmithwriter.com

If

By Rudyard Kipling (abridged)
If you can meet with Triumph and Disaster
*   And treat those two impostors just the same;*
If you can bear to hear the truth you've spoken
*   Twisted by knaves to make a trap for fools,*

…If you can talk with crowds and keep your virtue,
*   Or walk with Kings nor lose the common touch,*
If neither foes nor loving friends can hurt you,
*   If all men count with you, but none too much;*
… Yours is the Earth and everything that is in it,
*   And, which is more, you'll be a Man, my son!*

DEDICATION

Yes, I believe in angels and my wife Rhea is the leader in this group. Without her, none of my successes would have occurred. She kept our home heaven and a haven for me.

My older daughter Robin was my medical school graduation gift that has kept giving, along with her husband Ross who were a delight to watch succeed and grow.

Debra came next and blossomed like a flower year after year, and with her husband Scott never have stopped bringing joy and happy surprises into our life.

Andy is my oldest grandson and became my friend; and for a short time, business partner. He continues to make me proud with his construction company success, but even more by marrying Erin and producing the first of the great grandchildren, Jacob.

Abigail is his sister, my oldest granddaughter. We smile when we see her accomplishments. I like to think I had a little influence in the direction of her career. She now is married to Darryl who is fun to be around.

Alexander is Debra's oldest. He probably understands the pleasure I have watching him grow professionally,because he is a master psychologist married to his partner Melissa. Alex listened to my music politely and then composed his own. His best production was Benjamin, our second great grandson.

Hello to Sarah, my youngest granddaughter, who makes the sun shine with her optimism and positive attitude. She knows more about "Poppy-spit" then the rest and now is entering a blossoming career.

WOW! Surrounded by angels.

TABLE OF CONTENTS

PROLOGUE: FOR THOSE TO COME

I've been a refugee, soldier, husband, father, doctor, lawyer and judge, indeed, and to the best of my knowledge, the only doctor-lawyer-judge in the United States. I've overseen or consulted in 15,000 malpractice suits, no other person has been involved as many in the United States. I've also been involved in over 300 malpractice trials, again, probably more than any other trial lawyer in the United States. I've had a good career and a wonderful life.

I've learned from the many remarkable people who have come into my life, the good and the bad. I also have a profound belief in angels; some may scoff at this – a judge who believes in angels? Perhaps we need more who believe in the intervention of the divine and that good is a greater force than evil, and that if you simply believe, and express gratitude, then more good will come into your life. Little else can explain my good fortune and the many times I, or those close to me, have inexplicably escaped harm. I am grateful for the angels in my life, those seen, and those unseen.

During this journey, I've also wondered whether G.P.S. means more than Global Positioning System. Could it also mean:

Good Parents and Spouse
Good Problem Solving
Good Product and Service
Good Planning and Study
Good Plans and Strategies

G.P.S. can be a pretty good guide. It relates to work too. You do some things well because you're expected to. Other times you achieve because you like doing it and you want to show off. Then you do something exceptionally well, and that isn't every day. To be exceptional one needs extra effort, extra thought, extra work, and a lot of good luck. Always try to do better than good. Excellence is memorable. And a person who is most often remembered is one who is honest, is mannerly, and has no bigotry.

My passion for work and success has been enabled by the love and support of my wife, Rhea who married me on December 26, 1954. Our wedding photograph shows me, as pleased as punch, in a suit with white tie, and Rhea in an organza cowl-neck wedding dress, with a bouquet of huge, pale orchids offsetting her dark beauty. She helped bless my life with children, grandchildren and great-grandchildren. We are partners in everything. When I had a medical practice Rhea worked in my office. When I went to law school, she went to paralegal school, and when I became a judge, she became my judicial assistant. Except when I am traveling, we are always together. It's the way it should be, but it only happens if you're lucky.

Ours is a very close family, and in addition to the narrative of my life, I want this book to be a way that my heirs can know and understand their family history and legacy. There is value in knowing ancestral history and in learning how the past may impact the future. But most of all I hope to continue a dialogue with my family, those born and those yet to come, in some way from wherever time may take me.

I was always the family doctor, relied upon for medical care by every member of my family. My children, grandchildren and great-grandchildren are well-loved and they have paid me back five-fold with their love, understanding, and trust.

Whenever they were sick I was consulted. Because of my training and also because they knew how much I cared, I was their comforter. Sometimes they just needed to be assured that they would get well and that I could cure everything. I could cure a stomach ache. I could cure a rash. I could cure an infection.

And I sometimes would cure all these things with the same magic medicine. Now they are adults and they laugh at this, but the same magic medicine still works. What is it? It goes by the name of *Poppy Spit*.

Whenever they as children needed instant relief or immediate cheering up, I would put Poppy Spit on it. I would put Poppy Spit on any boo boo or sore throat or aching tummy, then sooth it, pamper it until it was dry, and they would know immediately that the magic medicine was providing relief.

That's what is called trust.

That's what is called a belief system.

That's what is called good medicine, because in fact, it works.

I cannot put into words how much my family means to me or the encouragement that I received from my family. My father taught me how to finish a job, how to learn mechanical skills, and how never to give up when the job became difficult. My mother gave me constant encouragement.

"You can do whatever you set your mind to do," she would always say.

She too expected me to finish a job. She always said that she knew I'd succeed.

I was most fortunate to have met my wife Rhea, who for sixty years has been the solid rock and conscience of our family. Though my stories might not reflect it, I had a desperate need for a conscience guide and she provided that admirably. She was always there for me and coming home to her was the highlight of every trip I made away from home. No matter how much enjoyment I derived from one of my trips, either business or pleasure, coming into the house and seeing her overshadowed everything else. And it continues to be that way.

We have two grown daughters, Robin and Debra, who themselves became proud parents and successful professionals. Robin married Ross Katzman. They work together as partner dentists. Of their children, Andrew is a successful builder, and Abagail is a talented cardiology nurse practitioner. Rhea and I are proud of the lives they are leading.

Debra married Scott Michaud and they built a magnificent law practice. As to their children, Alexander is a master psychologist and partners with his wife Melissa, and Sarah likely will be a nurse practitioner. Three of the four grandchildren are married, and our great-grand-children, Jacob and Benjamin, fit perfectly into our family of angels, people who give me much more love than anyone has a right to expect.

They literally and figuratively allow me to fly as high as I am able. It's as though they are all made of helium, lifting me to greater heights over a lifetime.

These are the angels on my shoulder who continually lift me. This book is written for my grandchildren and great-grandchildren, they have heard many of these stories and I hope that one day they will read this book to their children. I hope that it may be of value to others too.

CHAPTER 1

DO NO HARM

Doctors do not want to testify against other doctors, because word will get out, and no doctor, or any of his friends, will ever again refer a patient to the doctor who honors his patients and betrays his careless colleagues.

The original version of the Hippocratic Oath, first written by the Greek physician, Hippocrates, in the fifth century BCE, and which all doctors swear to uphold reads, in part, the doctor's responsibility to patients: "I will keep them from harm and injustice." The modern version, authored in 1948, and adapted by many medical schools globally, attests,

> *I will remember that there is art to medicine as well as science, and that warmth, sympathy, and understanding may outweigh the surgeon's knife or the chemist's drug.*
>
> *I will not be ashamed to say "I know not," nor will I fail to call in my colleagues when the skills of another are needed for a patient's recovery.*

I thought of all these things when a 23-year-old woman from Arkansas came to me for help. She was told by a doctor that the lumps in her breast were from her boyfriend squeezing too hard.

"Twenty-three-year-olds don't get breast cancer," he told her. "If you have cysts in your breast, they will go away."

He was wrong.

The cancer spread and nine months later she was close to death.

She went to one of the better breast cancer hospitals in St. Louis where the surgeon who examined her explained how challenging treatment was. She told her that she may feel very sick and even depressed, and that it would last for six months. The surgeon also told the patient that had this particular cancer been diagnosed properly when she first went to see her doctor, she wouldn't have had to go through all this.

She arrived in my office scared and confused, my challenge was how to get the surgeon to testify in court. In my years as the United States only medical doctor who is also a lawyer, and then a judge, I encountered this problem often. I was denounced by many doctors for my work in trying to get justice for patients.

In this case, as soon as I heard the surgeon's name, I felt some hope. I knew her years before when she was in medical school and I was finishing law school. I was selling my Gainesville condo, the base for my law school studies, and a medical student and his new bride, who was also a medical student came to look at it. I took pity on them. They had just moved to Gainesville, had no money, and I could see they really liked it, so I asked, "How much can you afford to pay a month?"

They could afford $300 a month. I let them have it for that. I didn't ask for a down payment. I told them as soon as they finished medical school and their residency and got jobs, the monthly payment would then go up to $1,400. They agreed, and after a number of years they paid off the condo, got divorced and went their separate ways. Fifteen years later, Suzanne, who had rented and bought my condo, was the chief of breast surgery in this St. Louis hospital.

When I approached her about the case, she said, "I can't help you. This is a referral. I don't like doing this. Testifying really interferes with a referral practice."

"You don't remember me, do you?" I asked.

There was silence and then she said, "Oh my word, Harry, I suddenly remember."

She remained reluctant to testify.

"I can't help," she said. "I can't testify in a malpractice case."

"Okay," I said, "Let's move on to the deposition that is being taken by the other side. They are going to develop a line of argument that things aren't as bad as Dr. Rein makes them out to be. They will say the patient would have ended up this ill because this is one of the worst cancers."

We proceeded to take her deposition. As she testified she began to cry. She said that the doctor who sent this patient to her had misdiagnosed the young woman and had doomed her to die a terrible death.

"I don't think anyone understands what a terrible condition this is," the surgeon said, "and how bad it's going to get. I hate to testify in these cases because of the horror. I try to keep all this information from my patients so they don't have emotional fear and anxiety before they die."

We won the case. But what were the odds that she would testify for me like that? About a million to one, because of a past kindness, I had pierced the shield.

Doctors Lie

Over the years, I have evaluated over 15,000 malpractice cases and attended more than 300 trials. Those experiences created a national reputation that has seen me aid lawyers and companies from over thirty states and five countries. My career testifying in malpractice cases extended from 1973 to 1983, even before I went to law school. Sadly, I heard testimony, read reports and witnessed courtroom behavior that the public would find hard to believe. Jurors believe that doctors will not lie and when there is disagreement, they tend to believe that the facts are so difficult that even the doctors can't reach accord and therefore no malpractice occurred. I have been told more than once, "Doctors don't lie, and if they disagree, how can we favor one side over the other?"

Do doctors lie? Yes, to try and get out of trouble. But most often it increases the trouble they are in. How often do they lie? From my experience I would say in almost every case. The defense usually ends up blaming the patient.

Doctors also lie because in many cases it's hard to prove the lie. Doctors will say, "I saw it, but I didn't write it. I can't write everything down. But I remember it this way."

Or a doctor will make up a diagnosis. One doctor testified that his patient was depressed, telling the court that "she told me terrible things about her family, and I wouldn't be surprised if her husband beat her. I didn't put it in the record, because we know how people can get in trouble when you write that."

Deception is not unusual. In tobacco cases, for instance, an entire industry lied for decades. Tobacco companies bombarded the public with advertising, even though they knew all along that smoking caused cancer. And if a patient sued, the defense was that patient could have stopped any time he wanted to. He was to blame.

Defining Malpractice

Today we keep malpractice issues a secret. All the public knows is that a patient is suing a doctor. From that bit of information anyone who reads that takes sides without knowing much more. I reduce malpractice prevention to one easy-to-understand sentence: *Do the right thing, at the right time, for the right reason, and if you do not get the expected result, find out why.*

If you're a mechanic and you're not careful enough to put all five nuts back on a wheel after you take it off to fix the tire, if you leave one loose because you're in a hurry and you don't care enough to do it right, you should never do that work again. If you're preoccupied and that gets in the way of delivering quality service of any kind, then you're at fault. That's the sum and substance of most malpractice cases. If a person isn't careful or if he doesn't care enough, it's dangerous. If someone knows he doesn't have enough information, and acts anyway, most of the time it will take care of itself. But in a rare case when it doesn't, then you have malpractice.

Malpractice is a combination of ignorance and laziness but the reaction is always an emotional one. Today's practice of medicine often leads to malpractice. Doctors are told to be busier by the corporations who own them, they then see more patients, and hurry through the examinations. They don't have time to listen. A patient who lies can sandbag doctors, because he or she is likely to miss hearing something important that the patient is telling him. That leads to litigation.

Inadequate communication leads to malpractice.

Also the doctor's failure to be honest with himself or the patient means he fails to ask: "Do I need to spend more time with this person? Do we need more time and effort to fix this or should we be superficial and just let it go, and hope it will correct itself?" These are at the core of medical malpractice.

In cases of collisions that cause serious injury, the defendant makes up the facts by saying, "The guy suddenly started backing up and I couldn't get away from him fast enough."

Sometimes the jury believes it.

I had one case, which was a combination of medical malpractice and a personal injury case. There was an awful car accident, where an oncoming truck tried to pass a slower car in front of it and crossed into my client's lane of traffic. He sped up to get back into his own lane, on a two-lane country road, but as he did this he sideswiped my client's car which was thrown into the ditch and rolled twice. One passenger was killed, another suffered multiple rib and extremity fractures, and a concussion. Dozens of large, color photographs of the crash scene were shown to the jury. The description of the crash and the injuries to the plaintiff were terrible. The question wasn't whether the plaintiff would collect, but how much.

The jury went out and after several hours came back. Its verdict: zero award. Everyone was shocked. Afterward, several members of the jury discussed their deliberations. One said, "It was the evidence of the person injured in the crash that caused us to vote against him. The pictures given to us by the plaintiff's attorney influenced us." The photographs gave multiple different views of the accident scene including the surrounding landscape. In one picture, lying on the ground outside the car, was a beer can. The jurors came to the conclusion that the plaintiff had been drinking, and so they weren't going to reward him for being hurt.

As it turned out, the plaintiff had not been drinking. The beer can be litter lying at the side of the road where the car rolled. But it was in the picture.

Jurors see and hear everything. Maybe one person will miss something, but there are twelve of them sitting there, and they will see and hear *everything*, including things that have nothing to do with the case. They see your demeanor, your behavior, how you walk, how you talk, how you dress, and how you behave. They listen to how you speak to the judge and watch how you address those with you, even when it's not part of the case. If you're a lawyer, you'd better look at those pictures closely yourself before showing them to the jury.

In the beginning

Malpractice may stem from an intervention or lack of intervention, doing something or not doing it, it may stem from poor planning or hurrying. Good medicine requires doing the right thing, at the right time, in the right way, for the right reasons. If a doctor does not get the anticipated result, he or she should check out why the anticipated result did not occur.

There were malpractice litigations back in the time of the Old Testament. But things really started to boil and bubble in the mid-1970s in the United States.

In January 1974, all the major newspapers reported that St. Paul, the largest malpractice insurance company in the country, had tripled its malpractice premiums for doctors. The medical profession responded angrily, some alleged that the reason St. Paul raised its rates was that it had just taken a major loss on the stock market. The noise over the huge raise in rates awakened the legal world to malpractice tort law. Patients realized they could sue. It educated the public that the quality of medical care could be judged by people who weren't physicians.

It has been said that when you let the camel's nose into the tent, you can never get the smell out. Secrets became public. Malpractice lawsuits increased every year until about 2010, when there was a sharp drop in medical malpractice litigation because many state legislators were persuaded by health care providers to control the cost of malpractice litigation. Personal injury cases have also swelled during that time frame.

A classic example was a rear-end car impact. The driver of the front vehicle says, "I have neck pain." A doctor puts a brace on his neck and tells him he needs three weeks of physical therapy. He gets a note that says he is disabled and he sues for damages. Suppose he isn't really hurt? How can the issue be resolved by the insurance company?

A caricature, oft-told in Florida from the early 1970s until about the mid-1980s, was that in South Florida a driver would hire a lawyer about an hour before his stated car accident. And yes, there was a lot of fraud in Florida before the no-fault law. As the family physician with the largest practice in central Florida I developed a relationship with insurance companies and lawyers to help them discern between true and false claims.

I became the regional advisor on medical issues for the Sears chain in central Florida too. All these events changed me from a family doctor known to continue making house calls to someone with an interest in the law. I wrote my first article, "The Medical Expert: Two People," which was published in *The Defense Law Journal*. In that article I suggested that insurance companies needed those with medical backgrounds to take depositions because they would know the right questions to ask.

I taught insurance companies not to believe everything that the plaintiff's physician said, because they often wish to help their patients and may exaggerate treatments. Conversely, some doctors dislike litigants so much that they will minimize the severity of an injury. I taught ways for companies to distinguish the difference.

I soon testified for the plaintiff's lawyers as an expert witness and published a book, *The Primer on Soft Tissue Injuries*. The more I saw failings in the medical knowledge lawyers had and which would enhance their ability to manage medically related cases, the more I believed I needed to learn more and teach more extensively; , and so I decided to go to law school. While in law school my wife, Rhea became very sick and needed surgery. A surgeon was recommended by a lawyer friend in Gainesville, which was where we lived while I studied. The surgeon was out of town, so I was turned over to his associate, who said, "Rhea has to have surgery tonight." She had her surgery, but by her fourth night in the hospital I could see she was desperately ill. I had the nurse call the surgeon, who said, "I will see her in the morning."

I had her call him again and state that he should not wait.

"I know what it is," he said. "She's on the right medication. I'll see her in the morning."

I examined my wife and found an abscess in the area of the surgery that needed to be cut and drained.

"Call him back," I told the nurse. "And tell him what I found."

"It doesn't need to be drained tonight," he barked. "I'm not coming in. Don't call me again. I'll see her in the morning."

I was furious and recognized this response as one of the reasons I was in law school. But what to do now, was the real issue. I could see surgical packs behind the nurses' station and asked for one to drain the abscess myself.

"Are you kidding?" the nurse said, "I don't want to get fired."

"Please give me the surgical pack," I said firmly. "If not, I will come around the desk, and I will take it, and I will use it. You can call the sheriff or the police. You can do whatever you want, but by the time they come, I'll be finished with what I have to do."

She had examined Rhea and knew I was correct and so she relented.

"I don't know what's going to happen, but let's go," she said.

She handed me the surgical pack and followed me into my wife's room where I performed the five-minute procedure to drain the abscess. After it was complete, I thanked her. I found the address of the doctor's partner who had just returned from his trip to France. I called him and he agreed to meet with me at his home.

It took about ten minutes to drive to his house. He opened the front door. I said, "The reason I'm here, is because I don't want my wife to die." I told him the chain of events. "Now do what you have to do," I said and left.

Within two hours a group of physicians of various specialties surrounded my wife in the hospital. They consulted and began intensive management.

Rhea still needed another operation. The next day the original surgeon performed the operation with our consent, and Rhea soon came home. Two weeks later when visiting the original surgeon, he apologized profusely and asked, "Am I going to be in your husband's book?"

She asked what he was talking about.

"He's writing a malpractice book isn't he?"

"Why don't you call him?" she said.

But he never did, and she never saw him again. My desire to right wrongs came from the experiences of my childhood; as I've aged I've realized that those early memories resonate no matter how old or wise we may become.

CHAPTER 2

VIENNA

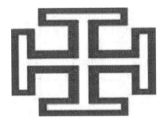

Mexico, 1938

Even now, when I look at this cross above my father's notes, I feel uneasy. Do I discern a swastika within this ancient cross? My father wrote long-hidden notes in German, his native tongue. He typed them on onion-skin paper in Mexico City in 1938, he was just twenty-nine. We don't know whether it was before or after Hitler's invasion of Poland in August of that year marking the start of the Second World War?

I am sure my father wanted to finish these notes but some pain is so deep that it defies return. Even I, anxious about their import and nervous about confronting his words, left them untouched for decades after his death. When, finally, I had the courage, and the need, to read them, I was older and he had been dead for decades. The paper was so fragile it was starting to disintegrate. I photocopied his notes and managed to darken fading type, and put them on sterner paper, before giving them to a translator.

I look again at the red cross. I should not feel such unease, this is after all a very old symbol, it was first drawn on Neolithic petroglyphs in

2,500B.C. The Ancient Persians used it as a sign meaning a magician or magi. In old Jerusalem it was gold upon a silver field, but the Nazi Reich liked it red. It became the symbol of the Austrofacist Federal State of Austria in 1934 led by Chancellor Engelbert Dollfus.

My parents were Austrian Jewish merchants, they were among the privileged of Europe in one of its most beautiful and intellectually gifted cities. This was the city of artist Gustav Klimt, psychologist Sigmund Freud, musicians Ludwig van Beethoven, Johann Strauss, Wolfgang Mozart, and Franz Joseph Hayden. When my parents lived in Vienna, a young engineer, Ferdinand Porsche, was fiddling with car designs.

Austria had a brief civil war between socialists and conservatives and although it led to bloodshed and loss of life, this was a city so refined and elegant it seemed nothing could remove the gild.

My father begins the three dozen page manuscript[i]; "On March 8, 1938 in Austria, then called the "Ostmark" there was an agitated feeling and nervousness in the air. The following Sunday, a national referendum [was to take place] to assess the trust for the government of Schusnigg, which existed since the assassination of the prior Chancellor Dr. Dollfuss [who] was assassinated in the Chancellery on July 15, 1934 by the German National Socialist Party [Nazi]. Two security organizations were founded: Homeland Security and the "Fatherland Front." In the next four years, the victims of these two organizations were the socialists and the Jews. Wherever possible, the former were suppressed and their rights were taken away by order of the government of Schuschnigg. Under such circumstances, the Nazis who were still illegal at the time, secretly grew in importance [through] many terror attacks and assassinations.

"Everyone had to join the "Fatherland Front" by November 1, 1937, whether he was willing or not, otherwise he was accused of high treason. I destroyed my I.D. card for the Social-Democratic Labor Party

---

i The full text of my father's letter is part of the addendum.

and on October 25, 1937, I joined the Fatherland Front. The political arena was tense and agitated. A climax was reached on March 8, 1938, when our Chancellor, Dr. Schuschnigg was due to speak. All of Austria was in feverish expectation. We sat around the loudspeaker and waited for a solution for the preservation of A u s t r i a.

"Finally, at ten after 8 o'clock our apprehensive waiting around the loudspeaker was over. Chancellor Schuschnigg announced that a referendum was to be held to show confidence for the government and against the Nazis. He and the audience chanted, 'Red-White-Red until Death,' the colors of the Austrian flag."

My father continued, "The following morning, walls were painted with this slogan, businesses and homes had their flags out, Red-White-Red. Cobblestones and sidewalks were painted with glossy red and white paint. Rich Jews collected 500,000 Austrian Shillings and chose three delegates from the Vienna Israelite Religious Community to personally deliver the monies to Chancellor Schuschnigg…"

"But, oh no, not even 48 hours later we had to listen to the Chancellor with a short speech in which he declared his resignation and with a nearly sobbing voice, he spoke loud and clear: 'God protect Austria.' At that moment all of us listening had tears in our eyes, perhaps because we knew that our sad fate was finally sealed.

"In his place, Dr. Seyss-Inquart, a Nazi, became Chancellor. On the 12th of March 1938 at six in the evening, the new Chancellor announced on the radio that the German troops were on their way from the 3rd Reich and were already marching into Austria. He pleaded with the Austrian population not to put up any resistance.

"Surprisingly, when the German forces moved across the Austrian borders into the provinces, they were greeted by large crowds with jubilation and songs. They shouted "Heil Hitler" with much gusto! Patriotism disappeared from the hearts of all – the true soul showed itself. Were almost all Fatherland fraudsters instead of Homeland protectors? Now they shouted with utmost force: 'Heil Hitler!'

"Hitler and his followers marched through the provinces and cities of Austria. On the next day, it was a Saturday, he concentrated his troops and led them into Vienna, arriving in the center of the city by noon. He sent 200 airplanes that crossed over the city for two hours at very low altitude to scare the population. Finally, the German military forces entered the city with a great parade, songs and whistling. There were 300,000 solders. Schools and municipal buildings had to be vacated to house the military."

My father's papers tremble in my hands as I sit back and go into the memories of a little boy. This is what I remember. Silence had replaced joy at 23 Glockengasse, Wien. My parents, Sam and Berta Rein, were whispering a lot. Something was going on they didn't want me to know. I was six and had just learnt how to read and write. My home had been cheerful and happy, but things were changing.

In the past I was allowed to cross the street by myself to visit Omama, my grandmother, who lived on the third floor of a small building. There was a grocery store on the ground floor, and whenever I visited, the young man who worked there would give me a piece of candy. Now I was told I could no longer cross the street or even go outside alone. My parents loved walking in the streets in the evening to look in the shop windows and go into the stores. They didn't do that anymore either.

They were afraid.

It was puzzling to a small child. How can it be that our parents, the most powerful people in the world, are fearful? A child observes but says nothing; the questions are there but too hard to form.

One afternoon in late March, 1938, after Germany annexed Austria, my parents and I gazed from our living room window as throngs of people filled the sidewalks, screaming with happiness and waving at hundreds of soldiers who goose-stepped down the street. Everyone was saluting and yelling, "Heil Hitler." My parents and I silently watched. They kept me very quiet, and then not being able to watch any longer, took me away from the window. It wasn't long after that the Nazis and the Austrians who supported them started doing everything they could to humiliate the Jewish citizens of Vienna.

The takeover of our country by the Nazis was called the *Anschluss*. People were celebrating because Austria once great, had been a small, powerless country, and now it could be a great country again, thanks to Hitler and the Nazis.

The Nazis began their assault on the Jews as part of a strategy called *Jeudenfrei* (free of the Jews), which they extended to Austria, Hitler's birthplace. In my father's notes, he described it thus, "All Austrian Nazis promptly got their uniforms and weapons, even if they had not reached their 18th year. You saw youth running around on the street with weapons who acted importantly [even though] "snot was still running from their noses."

"All cars of Jewish owners were 'acquired.' Jewish business people were arrested. All Jewish municipal institutions and buildings were vacated and destroyed and in their place, horse stables, living quarters and barracks were built. Jewish temples were destroyed. The prayer books and Torah were piled in large heaps and burnt. Jewish shops were plundered to the last nail – larger businesses were immediately transferred to Aryan (non-Jew) hands. Later on, the front of any Jewish shop was sentineled, not letting any Aryan customer enter the store. Every passer-by was asked whether he was Jewish. If so, he would have to position himself in front of the store, holding a big board that read: 'Don't buy anything from this Jewish Pig.'"

Torture

My father's notes tell of Jews being forced to clean cars and windows. "Many were forced to swallow the soap that was left over – or if you refused to do so, you were beaten. On the street, Jews were gathered up and transported in extra-large cars and trucks, like cattle, [for some] the trip went a little further, and that was the concentration camp D a c h a u.

"My brother and I had a clothing shop. The clothes were made by us. We employed about fifty people. Twenty were employed in our own workshop that was located separately from the storage and showroom. Hardly eight days had gone by after the so-called seizure of power, when a tailor by the name of W. came to us with a group of S. S. men and the Bezirksverwalter, or district administrators of the Storm Troopers and demanded retroactive payment of wages for the last two years because of alleged underpayment.

"The District Administrator asked where the cash register was. We said that we do not have a cash register and have no money. A thorough search by six men followed. They ripped apart bedding, cut open feather and cloth ends suspecting hiding places for money or jewelry, and after less than an hour they found the hiding place of our personal effects. The next day, [storm troopers] appeared and confiscated our car."

The tailor who complained, spread dissent resulting in three tailors seizing my father's business. My father wrote, "There was no sight any longer of the 'Vienna heart' they were like beasts, even worse, a beast when full with food and drink becomes mild but the devil got into these people. Like a volcano lets its lava stream out, that's how they let their hate and bloodlust stream out to their fellow human beings, the J e w s. No one was exempted."

On one occasion my father and his brother were taken to a mansion that now housed the S.S. They were forced to scrub the ancient floors of the cellar. He wrote, "These jobs were always carried out under supervision of an S. S. man who always carried a stick in his hand in case he had to chastise us, perhaps for not working fast enough or, perhaps, he just felt like it. Sometimes he left his supervisory post and went to the upper level for some time since he was craving Schnapps like his other buddies who were already in the process of getting seriously drunk. Once, I used this opportunity to look around to see where screaming was coming from that we heard continuously.

"I saw in another room a man in his 40's, probably a physician, since he wore a white coat, lay on the floor and above him knelt an S. S. man who also carried a stick. He beat on the physician continuously with these words: 'Dirty Jew. Jewish Pig. Shout out with loud voice that you are a Jew.' This physician was obstinate and shouted with a hoarse voice, since he had been mistreated for quite a while, 'I a m a G e r m a n.'

"He had barely finished his exclamation and the cane beatings came down on him like hailstones. My blood started boiling, I wanted to help the man, but it became clear that it would surely mean my death, since I am a prisoner here also.

"Passing a closed door, I saw, peeking through the keyhole, a well-dressed lady trying to wash mountains of dishes that had come down from the feasting. I could see from the work that was in front of her that she could not manage that, shortly before we left the house, she collapsed."

For five hours my father and brother scrubbed the floors, then were made to walk around Vienna putting up Nazi posters. They were then taken back to the mansion where his brother was assaulted by an S.S. commandant who told my father and his brother that they owed their workers more money and should return the next day with receipts to prove it had been paid.

My father's brother and his wife immediately left the country. Two days later my father's passport that he'd applied for a month before arrived. "But the passport alone was not enough to leave, you also had to have additional papers from government agencies, such as a tax certificate, customs papers and a certificate of Good Conduct, etc. etc. Finally, you had to have a visa for a foreign country – that was the most important thing. We chose May 12, 1938, at 9 o'clock at night to escape with the aid of the same two men who helped my brother and sister-in-law escape.

"Because the escape was to go via a small lake with a tiny canoe, there was no possibility to have more than one small suitcase. According to our plan, my brother was to inform me of the successful crossing by a telegram that read: *Congratulations on your birthday.* It was to arrive at my house by 9:00 in the morning. If the crossing did not go well, there was to be no message.

"I waited in vain for news. It was 9:00, 10:00, 11:00 and noon. I became quite worried. I got hot, I got cold, my head worked feverishly as to what I should do. I sent my wife to different consulates to try and get visas for us for whatever country, be it forever, be it for the other end of the world or for just a few weeks, valid for any border country just to get us going today. I knew there was an impending catastrophe coming our way. Via a friend, a friend only because of money, a high-ranked official with the S. S., we finally acquired a visa at 3:00 o'clock in the afternoon for a great amount of money. What did money or goods matter in such a case, since you could not take either along?

This man brought the visa to the shop, my wife was with him in his car. On the way, he said to my wife several times she should hide her head so that no one would see that he was in the car with a Jewish woman as he would be in danger of losing his job and as functionary of the S. S. he could be sent to the concentration camp.

"As a "friendship reward" he left my house, heavily loaded with monies and goods.

"At 4:00 o'clock in the afternoon, two men came from the Gestapo and asked for my brother. I told him I did not know where he was. They continued: "We have learned that you want to emigrate, is that true?" and I answered: "Yes, as soon as I receive permission from the government and have the necessary papers."

"'Where is your passport that we issued to you a little while ago," one asked.

"'My wife has that passport," I said.

"'Good" said the officials "we will come back tonight at 7:00 o'clock. Prepare all the documents for us in the meantime, including the passport."

"I knew that no time was to be lost. Quickly, I gathered our business journals and locked the shop and workshop and threw away the keys.

"Off we went to the railroad station without any good-bye to my mother or my siblings. Before the train left, I telephoned my sister and asked her to please speak to my mother and ask her forgiveness.

"We had hardly reached the Czech border when a German official in civil clothing came into our compartment and asked whether I had a brother and what his first name was? I guessed that my brother and his wife were caught when they tried to illegally cross the border.

"'Where are you traveling to?' asked the official. I told him I was traveling to the spa resort Pystian for treatment because I suffer from rheumatic pain and since I never travel far or near without my wife and child, I brought them with.

"'Do you suffer from the same illness as your brother? You do not look sick at all,' he said." My father told him that the illness was hereditary. My parents and I were put off the train and sent to a "revision hall" for questioning and to be searched, this included ripping the seams of their garments in search of money or jewels. They found none.

My dad picks up his pen and continues, "It was already 10:30 at night. My child lay on a bench and slept, protected by a Czech woman who had just visited her husband, a border employee who was at work at that time. The Czech officials were annoyed by the Germans bad treatment of us.

"I saw that one of the [senior Czech] border employees and a Gestapo man get into a heated argument that ended with the Czech impressing their stamps [on my dad's passport]. This was not one second too early, as the stationmaster was about to give the starting signal for the train waiting there. This was 1:45a.m. We jumped from the bench, thanked the Czech officials and for the next half hour we were unable to speak because of fear, joy, surprise and heart-pounding, as the train traveled through Czech lands."

That train turned out to be the last the Nazis permitted to leave Austria carrying Jews.

The diaspora

My father's experience as a menswear manufacturer stood him in good stead, he got work sewing. When we heard that the Nazis were coming to Czechoslovakia, we fled to Zagreb, Yugoslavia, only to see the Yugoslavs become friends with the Nazis. The threat was always the same if you were Jewish: if you don't leave now, you face the wrath of the Nazis.

Yugoslavia began repatriating Jews back to Germany. They said, "We don't want you, we're sending you back." I got whooping cough. Nobody wanted to go near a kid with whooping cough because it was highly contagious. The officials said, "Get him out of here. Send him to the seashore." It was believed that sea air could heal whooping cough.

Across the water was Italy. It was my father's goal that we end up there. One day he disappeared. He snuck into Italy. When he returned he said, "The Italians don't want us either. They want to kill us too."

Our situation and that of millions of other European Jews, was dire. I remember a lot of bus rides, and at the end of 1938 we ended up in southern France, where somehow we bought tickets in steerage class to the United States America on a great ocean liner, the *Ile de France*. We were in steerage, accommodation shared with cargo. There were very poor toilet facilities, and pots and pans for ablutions. I slept in a bunk with my parents. Once a day we were permitted to go above deck for a couple of hours.

One day on the deck my parents met Joseph Kutcher, principal of a high school in the Bronx and Rose Shapiro, assistant principal. They had been vacationing in France and were now returning to New York in cabins some floors above our cheap accommodation.

Joe and Rose took a liking to my parents and me. They listened to the story of how we traveled from country to country to escape the Nazis.

"When you come ashore in the United States," they said, "You'll love it. You can be happy. Whatever's going on in Europe is not really our concern; we know it's serious, but it'll be over soon." Everyone thought that in the U.S. In my journey through life, I have recognized that wishful thinking rarely works, but diligence and thoughtful intervention is what should motivate us. This is as true in medicine, law, and jurisprudence, as it is in international affairs.

Ellis Island

My father was sure that when we got off the ship at Ellis Island, go into New York City. get a job, and everything would be okay. He was wrong. After seven days in the dark bowels of that big liner, we landed at Ellis Island, only to learn we would not be allowed to get off the ship. The United States, it seemed, was anxious to not admit any more refugees, including Jews, and invoked a quota that existed. Those who were admitted had to show they would not be a financial burden. The Great Depression of the 1920s and '30s lingered. You had to prove that you were a professional, a doctor or a lawyer, or you had a job waiting for you, or a relative living in the country had to guarantee that they would subsidize you to the tune of twelve dollars a week.

My father didn't have a profession and he had no money. My mother had two uncles living in New York, and she knew their addresses. My parents were certain they would take us in or give us a job.

The officials at Ellis Island called them on the phone.

"Bertha and Sam Rein are here with their son," the official said.

"That's nice," said her uncles.

"Could you guarantee then twelve dollars a week?"

"No."

"Why not?"

"We have a lot of family and we have enough trouble supporting them."

"If you don't support them, they will be sent back," they were told.

"Yeah, that's sad," was their answer.

No one came forward to help us. In time to come, when we arrived in America, my mother renewed her relationship with them, in good part because we were so poor. She relied on them for hand-me-down clothing for me. I never had a new piece of clothing except for socks and underwear until I was 16. And so my mother tried not to show her bitterness, but it was there, it was always there, beneath her smiles and expressions of gratitude for their castoffs.

When I was 16 and the great day came for me to get my first new suit of clothes my father took me to a menswear store in lower east side New York where the poor shopped. In those days in that part of town bartering was expected. My dad haggled to get the price down to $14 for the suit. As we walked away I asked, "How did you know to stop at $14?"

My dad said, "When I saw him reach into his pocket to switch his hearing aid off."

But on that day on Ellis Island when my mother's cousins consigned us to a miserable end at the hands of Nazis, Joseph Kutcher and Rose Shapiro were with us when that news came. They couldn't believe our flesh and blood could be so heartless. Joe and Rose were very upset. We were going to get sent back, and who knew what was going to happen? Another ship, The St. Louis, with a boatload of Jewish refugees, was sent back to Europe. Lots of Jews on that ship ended up in South France, and most of them died in concentration camps run by the Nazis and French Nazi sympathizers.

We were given the choice of sailing to Cuba, which was taking Jews. We ended up in Havana. Not too long afterward the Cuban government started sending Jews to other Central and South American countries, which is how so many Jews settled there in the 1930s. I don't recall how long we lived in Cuba, it was just a few weeks, but the next thing I knew we were on a boat headed for Vera Cruz, Mexico, and ultimately Mexico City.

My father found work with a Jewish manufacturer of socks who spoke Yiddish. My father learned Spanish quickly and was given the job of managing the employees of the factory. My father was very well liked. He didn't know how to have an enemy.

In Mexico you could come in and open a business, but if you were not a professional you couldn't legally be an employee. Every Friday when my father got paid, there was a policeman waiting to take thirty percent of his pay to look the other way. He was happy to have a job so paid the cop, and went home.

I went to school in Mexico City, and learned Spanish quickly. We lived in Mexico City for three years. During this time my parents were writing to Rose and Joe, who immediately after witnessing how we were treated and dangers we barely managed to avoid, started a fundraising drive to bring us to the United States.

"If their family doesn't treat them right," they said, "then our school should. I want you to start saving pennies. Tell your parents that whenever they have a few extra pennies to send them with you to school." For three years they saved pennies and nickels, until they had enough money to buy us visas and bus tickets from Mexico City to New York City. We should recall that 1938 to 1942 were not easy times for many people.

CHAPTER 3

MOCKY AND THE GANG THAT COULDN'T SHOOT STRAIGHT

The bus trip from Mexico City to New York lasted seven days and nights. We ate bananas and hot dogs. We drank Coca-Cola. We arrived in Williamsburg, Brooklyn just before the Pearl Harbor attack of December 7, 1941. We spoke only German and Spanish but that, fortunately, did not prove a hindrance. My father got a job stuffing feathers into pillows. He was paid $12 for a sixty-hour week. My mother mopped floors in a Hebrew day school. Rose and Joe remained our friends and when I got married in 1964, they came to my wedding. Rhea still joyfully uses the serving dishes they gave us.

I attended P.S. 16 on Wilson Street in Williamsburg. I didn't speak English, so I was put in the first grade, even though I should have been in the fourth grade. The first grade teacher liked me, so with her extra help I learned English quickly. She recognized that I should not have been placed in so low a grade. She told me she would promote me to the third grade as soon as I learned fifty words of English and could respond to some simple questions in English.

I learned to read English pretty quickly and it didn't take long for her to promote me. My new teacher continued to give me extra attention and helped me succeed. I liked school, but at least once a week I would get beaten up, because I was a foreigner.

I lived in a mixed neighborhood of mostly Irish and Italian Catholics. There were Orthodox Jews and non-orthodox Jews. The kids called me *mocky*, it meant pest or plague, and was used to describe a refugee Jew who spoke poor English or a Jew who was looked down upon as "unsophisticated" or "low class." Decades later the memory of those insults still hurt. I was smaller than the kids my age and so I was also called a sissy boy. Some wither under insults, but in me it bred ambition, and one day, I vowed to myself, I'll show them all. I was not good at sports and was always clean so some kids would beat me up, and when I got home, my clothes would be torn or dirty, and if I was dirty, my mother would also beat me up.

After school I would try to disappear, but it wasn't easy. I do not remember Brooklyn fondly. In Williamsburg, my friends and classmates became either a professional, a gangster, or ended up in jail, or dead. I don't know anyone who became a plumber, a cab driver, a janitor, an office manager, or a salesperson. Most of my friends were Jewish, but I also had a lot of Italian friends. The apartment house in which I lived contained Polish people, black people, orthodox and ultra-orthodox Jews, Puerto Ricans, any nationality and background you can think of. When you talk of the American melting pot, I lived in a good example.

I became adept at studying people. The two poolrooms in Williamsburg were a good place to start. One of them, Maxie's, was where only the good people went. Maxie sold salami sandwiches for a nickel, and it was clean. There was no gambling. Maxie didn't put up with any nonsense.

The other poolroom was on Roebling Street, and it was where all the bad dudes and the gangsters congregated to gamble. My mother told me, "If you go into that poolroom on Roebling Street, I will break both your legs." Every time I passed by I was tempted to go in. I only went in once and immediately felt fear. The temptation was met, but my conscience was too strong.

I enjoyed playing pool at Maxie's. I was a good enough pool player that I was able to double my allowance, and this meant I could go to the movies every once in a while.

The most famous denizens of my neighborhood were the Gallo brothers, Joey and Bobby. The other famous person from the neighborhood was Alan Dershowitz who became a well-known Harvard attorney. Alan lived around the corner, he wasn't anyone of any significance then, but Joey Gallo and his two brothers were.

Every week I had to pay Joey Gallo a dime for protection. Those who wouldn't pay got the hell beat out of them. And so I paid. I know of people who refused to pay and were taken to the door of the basement of the Gallo's home, and when they opened the door, the old lion they kept in the basement would roar, probably as a plea to escape, but children didn't know that, and so they paid the Gallo's. In years to come we discovered the lion was toothless, but not then, so I paid my dime, and that was that.

When I was growing up, any time I faced a physical challenge or was at a disadvantage, I would withdraw into study or work. I'd take a detour rather than be confrontational. I didn't realize it until many years later, but this was the way of the Holocaust survivor. You avoid danger or powerful people who could physically hurt you. I never wanted to put myself in a position where I could be put down violently. It was a behavior I learned from my parents. My mother wanted to be liked by everyone. She was also afraid of everything because of what happened in Vienna. My mother taught me that it was good was to have people like you,

My father, like my mother, avoided conflict. If ever I had a disagreement with anyone, he'd tell me, "Just leave it alone. Ignore it. Walk away. It'll go away." I vowed there would come a time when I wouldn't avoid conflict just because my father did. I admired Uncle Alfred who wasn't afraid no matter what, or so it seemed.

California

After Pearl Harbor, the United States started conscription. If your wife was pregnant or if you had more than one child, you didn't have to go. My father said, "We all live in this country and you shouldn't try to shirk your duty," and so he enrolled in the military. My two uncles, Alfred, a clothing manufacturer, and Paul, a furrier, spent the war becoming very wealthy. My father was assigned to the Seabees, the construction battalion of the Navy. That's not where he wanted to go, but that's where he was sent. The proudest day of his new life came when he put on his military uniform and became a citizen of the United States. He made me a uniform identical to his, and when he was on leave he and I would walk on the streets proudly wearing our uniforms.

My father was stationed in California. He sent home the twenty-three dollars a month that we lived on. I didn't know much about the war. My mother wasn't politically inclined. All I knew was that there was a war and my father was in the Navy.

In January 1944, just before my father was due to be shipped out to the Pacific, I became ill. It started with strep throat and developed into scarlet fever. At that time there was no penicillin[1]. Our doctor was a kind man who my mother adored. I remember the doctor coming to our home, and my mother crying because I had scarlet fever and there was no medicine for it. In those days a lot of people died of the disease. My mother called either the Navy or the Red Cross, and they contacted my father. They said, "Sam, your son is sick. He's going to die. You'd better get home."

They took him off the ship and sent him by train back home to Brooklyn. It took him three or four days. When he arrived home he was ready for the worst, because they thought I was dying, but as soon as he

---

1 Although penicillin was discovered by British researcher, Alexander Fleming in 1928, it only went into commercial production in March, 1944, when Pfizer started producing it in Brooklyn, NY.

walked in the door, my sore throat and my fever disappeared, and my scarlet fever went away. I was fine. The fever just broke, which is what it does. I got better, and my father was home for a week.

The ship that left for the Pacific without him was torpedoed. He returned to California, and a few months later was discharged and came home.

CHAPTER 4

IN THE REPAIR BUSINESS

When I was in the eighth grade I was chosen as one of two vale-dictorian candidates. The other boy and I had to write an essay about the United Nations and make a presentation. I felt that I was expected to say the United Nations was the most wonderful thing since sliced bread. I didn't think it was. I don't like doing what I'm supposed to do, just because it is a rule or customary. If it is unworthy and I can substitute something better or more valuable, I will. And so all my life I have been a pain in somebody's "rule." I learned about which countries were in the United Nations, and I knew that not all had helped Jews, and so my paper was, "Why the United Nations isn't great and why the United States shouldn't join it." The other student wrote his paper praising the United Nations, and so he was named the valedictorian.

I won the prize in mathematics and English, yet he was the vale-dictorian and almost seventy years later, the memory is bittersweet. My English teacher, sensing my disappointment, encouraged me to read poetry. I was reluctant until I found Rudyard Kipling's *If,* I suppose I have read it 200 or 300 times, I memorized it and still often draw on it.

As talented as I was academically, I was not good at sports, especially team sports. As a youngster my father taught me how to swim and to roller-skate. Later in life I learned snow skiing and have skied at dozens of locations. I just wasn't good when strength, rather than skill and technique, were needed.

I could excel if someone wanted me to do something special or different, or if they needed strategic input. When I was told, "You can't do that," I would question why not. My life's pleasure was meeting challenges. I was a high achiever as a boy, but I wasn't someone who could go to Coney Island, sit on the beach and suntan. There was always so much more to do. I always worked. My uncle Paul was a furrier in Brooklyn and my mother was a seamstress for him, as an example. My uncle's company would take in old coats as trade-ins. My job was to remove the lining without damaging it, so that the undamaged part of the lining could be used in smaller coats as new lining. I had a razor blade and my job was to cut the seams without cutting the lining. It was my first lesson in recycling.

I also delivered groceries for the grocer on the ground floor of my building. No salary, all I earned was tips. People didn't tip back then. They just said thank you, because the delivery was part of the service.

I would politely say, "Is that all?"

They would say, "Yes, that is all."

At that time, you could get two cents deposit return for a soda bottle and three cents for a milk bottle. And so I would ask, "Do you have any bottles I could take back?"

"Yes, you can have all my bottles," the customer would say, and that would serve as my tip. I made good money bringing those bottles back to the grocery store. The grocer would also give me any orange crates I needed for my scooter manufacturing enterprise. I was about 14-years-old. I would attach discarded roller skates onto boxes and I would sell them as scooters for seventy-five cents.

Earning a few cents was more important to me than sports; so if I was chosen for a sports team, which was unusual, I walked away because I didn't want to take the time from my studies or from my jobs. I wasn't willing to give up my afternoons just for fun.

I was almost sixteen when I entered Brooklyn Technical High School in 1947. It wasn't an easy school to get into but my math's scores and teacher praise paved my way. I was an important member of the Brooklyn Tech math team. We won first prize in New York City, not bad for kids from a poor neighborhood. But even though I was academically gifted, they still wanted me to take part in sport.

I can remember in gym class being asked to get up on the horse apparatus. I can remember saying, "Me, get on that? Are you kidding?"

I was still paying the Gallo brothers ten cents a week extortion. I took the trolley to school and back, and when I got off the trolley one Friday, Bobby Gallo, the older brother, would be waiting for me. He would demand his dime. I was ashamed I was paying them, and I vowed that I would no longer live in like my mother and father. One day when I was sixteen something came over me. I beat the hell out of Bobby Gallo. Bobby started pushing, shoving, and hitting me, and I kept swinging. I punched him in the face. His face was bruised and my clothes were dirty because we had been rolling around on the ground. When I got home, my mother was furious because not only were my clothes dirty, but I had gotten in a fight with the dreaded Gallo's. Her fear was that now the whole gang would come after me. All because I refused to pay that damn dime. So she let me have it too.

There may have been something to my mom's fears. Decades later a book and a movie was made about the three Gallo brothers, it was called, *The Gang That Couldn't Shoot Straight*. I've watched that movie at least four times. They also made it into the movie, *Goodfellas*. The Gallo boys were part of the Profaci family, which was part of the feared Colombo Mafia family. Years later he was one of those detained after the shooting of mafia kingpin, Joe Colombo, although Jerome A. Johnson, posing as a journalist, pulled the trigger, conspiracy theories still reign that this was a mob hit.

Joey Gallo, who some called Crazy Joe Gallo, would go onto create one of the bloodiest mob conflicts since the 1931 Castellammarese Mafia War. It led to Joey's murder in a clam restaurant after an all-night celebration of his birthday in April 1972. If you think of the restaurant shooting in *The Godfather*, then you know what happened. Bob Dylan immortalized him as a Robin Hood in his song, *Joey*, but Joey was always more about robbin' the hood, than a hero. Bobby Gallo, who by that time was part of the Genovese mafia family, was arrested in 2000 as part of a $50m FBI bust of stock exchange swindlers.

After throwing punches at Bobby Gallo I knew I had to change my after-school routine. After the school day ended, I would stay in school an hour and a half to two hours later. I made use of that time, studying and being involved in extracurricular activities. I took extra classes and graduated fourth in my class with all kinds of scholarship offers.

I never saw the Gallo's again. I knew the possibility existed that they could have been lurking behind any corner, but they were too busy collecting from other kids to bother with me. If they didn't see you for a couple of weeks, they forget about you.

When I was about sixteen, I began delivering telegrams by bicycle for Western Union in the afternoons and every weekend. I was earning well; thirty-five cents an hour, plus any tips I could persuade people to give. I felt wealthy. I did that job until I graduated high school. During time off and holidays, I went to work for my Uncle Alfred. He had a factory near Fifth Avenue in Manhattan that made pants for the military. He made khakis and chinos. He and his wife, my Aunt Peppi, taught me business practices and how to manage employees. My first job was to clean and sweep, and pick up pants, in other words, to keep the factory clean. At first when I was finished, I just stood and waited, looking to be told what else to do. My aunt would walk up to me and very pleasantly say, "What's the matter? Don't you see other things to do?" Because, she knew, there was always something to do. It was a loving lesson.

"Don't stand around," she'd say. "This is work time."

Later in my medical practice, I would use that same technique with my staff. When the nurses would just stand around between patients, I knew the rooms needed cleaning and the pills needed to be counted and packaged. I would smile and say, "What's the matter? Is there nothing else to do?" It worked. Thank you, aunt Peppi.

My uncle taught me something else. Don't use insults. Criticism must be turned into a teaching moment. Don't put someone down; raise them up higher.

Pants were cut in a specific way. You would lay out the cloth, back and forth, back and forth over a table that was about twelve feet long and four feet wide. A pattern would be drawn on the top with chalk, and you were to take a large circular saw to cut through twelve inches of cloth and follow the pattern.

It was a job that required focus and a steady hand. One day he said to me, "I think you're ready." He laid out the cloth and he said, "Go ahead and cut." I started cutting, and proud of my elevation I cut carelessly. I cut right across the leg, which meant I had ruined about fifty or sixty pairs of trousers. I wanted to disappear.

He must have been furious, but remained sympathetic. "You know," he said, "It ain't bad what you just did. We're going to make a lot of shorts, aren't we?"

The next day he asked me to try it again.

This time I did it perfectly.

Here was a man, who, instead of saying to me, "Dummy, you really screwed up. We don't need people like you here. Good bye," he talked to me compassionately and gave me everlasting confidence.

Another time I went right through the power cord with a saw. The power cord was about an inch-and-a-half thick filled with cable wires. He said, "You're going to become an electrician today, huh? Go fix it." Fixing something, almost anything, was not a chore for me. My father was mechanically inclined and if something was broken, he could fix it. He would say to me, "Come. We'll fix it together." We took apart clocks and watches. He built things out of scrap wood. As a result, I'm a fixer.

Years later when I built my dream house, I wired the twelve phone system, installed the hi-fi, and all the video.

The Help Squad

My English teacher suggested I become a tutor. Only a few years earlier I had been a child who had come to the country speaking no English, and now I was being asked to tutor English and mathematics, so I joined what was called the Help Squad. Boys would stay after school, and I would help them learn. I was able to help about fifteen students after school. The teachers who ran the Help Squad said to me, "You're good at teaching. You're going to have to do something where you incorporate that into your life's work. It's not engineering, or physics. Don't even think about being an actuary. Think about what you could do to help other people."

My mother said, "By paying close attention to others you can see what they are doing well, and then try to do it better." Those were all teaching moments.

And so with the words of those I respected still in my ears, I accepted a scholarship to the New York University downtown campus at Washington Square. I had no diversions when I was in college. I didn't go to parties, didn't join a fraternity, didn't drink, and didn't gamble. I got on the subway and went to school, got on the subway and went to work, got on the subway and went home to study. I did that every single day except at weekends. Most people think of college as pleasant. NYU wasn't pleasant. My time there was more like a sentence that had to be served.

And then I met Rhea Lutzker, a dark-haired good looker who was wise beyond her years. She became my girlfriend and later my fiancée, then my wife, my partner in business, lover, and a mentor and guardian of my conscience. The latter probably saved me a lot of grief. My parents and hers, Leon and Sarah Lutzker, owned summer cottages at Lake

Hiawatha, New Jersey, and that's where we met, on a double date when we were dating other people. Neither of us liked the person we were with, but we enjoyed each other's company. I had a summer job driving a twelve-passenger school bus from Brooklyn and Queens to camp in Jones Beach on Long Island. It provided me with transportation from New Jersey to New York and the camp paid for the gas. I drove Rhea to school each morning on my way to work, and picked her up each evening going home. That was an hour ride on Route 46 through to the Lincoln Tunnel and another hour on the Belt Parkway We talked about everything.

Other than falling in love, I have amnesia about college. I do remember that I never got a grade lower than an A in mathematics, until I took integral calculus my second semester freshman year. My second day of calculus I tried to learn a formula and found that I couldn't. I was blocked so completely I don't even remember what the formula looked like. That was very unusual for me. The fear I felt, the panic, which I can recall to this day, changed me. I decided mathematics wasn't for me. Maybe a nice Jewish boy should be a doctor, I thought. It's what every Jewish mother said, including mine. My one reservation was that I didn't like some of the doctors I had met. They seemed to lack a sincere liking for people. That did not make sense, but as I watched their behavior I noticed that they wanted everyone to think they were better – not because of their professional work results, but because of their title. They were snobs and acted as if they were above those around them. They were very supercilious, and I vowed that was not going to be me.

And so I set out to learn how to fix people. I was back in the repair business

While I was going to college I worked as an orderly. I thought if I didn't like being an orderly, I certainly wouldn't like being a doctor. I took a course to become an x-ray technician and quickly became certified. I took the jobs no-one wanted - an x-ray technician on night call and an orderly during the day - most weekends while in college, for seventy-five cents an hour. I carried bedpans and I gave enemas. I was a great enema giver; at that time enema therapy was very popular.

After a year I thought to myself, "This has been mighty good fun," and decided to pursue medicine.

Years later I read *Vernon Can Read!* by Vernon Jordan, one of President Bill Clinton's lawyers. He tells how he got a job in Washington, D.C. with one of the top law firms and rose to become a managing partner. He was black and from the Deep South in a pale-skinned corporate world. Racism was covered by only the thinnest of veils. "When I got the job, I was always the first one at work and I never left the office until everyone else had gone. I worked twice as hard as everyone else. And then I made the people working under me do the same thing." His story was so like mine.

I told Vernon Jordan's story to my grandsons. When my grandson, Andrew was sixteen, he worked as a busboy at a local restaurant. He loved his job because his share of the tips was in cash and he didn't have to wait until the end of the week for a paycheck. He came home the first night and said to me, "Grandpa, look at the money I made today. And I'm folding it the same way you do." He showed it to me, with the twenty on top and then a five and a couple of ones.

"You're not doing it the way I do it," I said. "Put the twenty on the inside and the ones on top."

"Why?" he asked. "I want to show that I have money."

"That's the whole point," I said. "The amount of money you have makes no difference in the way you treat other people. The only thing people care about is the type of person you are. If you show them how much money you have, they will dislike you."

A year later he said to me, "Grandpa, they made me a waiter."

"You can't be a waiter," I said. "You aren't eighteen yet. You can't serve alcohol until you're eighteen."

"Well, I'm a waiter," he said.

"Why would they have done that?" I asked.

"They like me," he said.

"They can't make you a waiter just because they like you."

"Someone else serves the alcohol, but they made me a waiter."

"How did you arrange that?" I asked.

In true Vernon Jordan style, he said, "Nobody likes to polish the glasses and put them away, so I come in early and polish the glasses before the waiters come in. And then I wait until the restaurant closed, and I put all the glasses away, so the waiters can go drink. I did their work for them, and so they really liked me and made me a waiter." My grandson made me proud. In his own way he emulated Vernon Jordan and me.

CHAPTER 5

A THIRST FOR KNOWLEDGE

Medical school admission was very difficult for Jews, there were thirty-five Jewish applicants for every Jewish student who was accepted. Today anyone who's academically qualified can get into medical school in the United States. There are three spots for every potential student. It wasn't that way when I was applying and it was even harder because I was applying after only three years of college. The good news is that I was accepted into two excellent medical schools overseas, the University of Lausanne in Switzerland and the University of Edinburgh in Scotland. The irony was that the medical school I really wanted to attend, the State University of New York was a subway ride away in Brooklyn. However, when I went for my interview I was told, "We would love to have you, but you need to go back to NYU and finish your senior year and then it's likely we'll take you." I felt another year of college would be a waste of time.

"I don't want to finish another year," I told the interviewer. "I'm going to medical school after three years."

"Well, not here," the interviewer said.

"I've already been accepted to Lausanne Medical School and the University of Edinburgh Medical School," I said, "but I really would prefer to go here. I live here. Your school is a great school and it isn't far from home. I really want to attend here."

It was a pleasant, polite interview, but basically the interviewer was saying to me, "Read my lips. Don't you know what no, means?"

He didn't know that I did not understand how to gracefully take no for an answer. I learned early on that if you are persistent while maintaining a friendly demeanor and a smile on your face, in many cases you can get your way.

"You know," I said, "I will be a great medical student. You will be very happy if you take me. I will be one of the best medical students you will ever have in this school if you accept me." This time, instead of no, he said, "We'll have to give it some thought." About six weeks later I received a letter of acceptance along with a full scholarship. A smile and persistence paid off.

I raced through college to get to medical school and now that I was in medical school I was determined to learn as much as I could in the four years allotted. To do this I developed my own curriculum in parallel with the regular courses I was required to take and learned in my own way. It didn't occur to me that anyone would notice, and if they didn't like it, I didn't care. Popularity was not a priority. Learning as much as I could was.

The lesson I took from medical school is this: discover what it is that you want to learn and figure out your own way to learn it. Everyone learns in a different way. If you try to learn everything they try to teach, you're going to miss half the things you want to learn. One great advantage I had was a nearly photographic memory. I was able to quickly distinguish what's important from what's not and to ignore the non-essential material. I could remember everything important and further, what book it was in, and what part of the page. If it was something important I'd say to myself: you better remember this and ten years later I could find it in the right book within twenty minutes.

I also memorized all the material I knew I would always need. I found that the medical school instruction routine was a hindrance to deep understanding of important issues and excess detail of rare issues.

My disdain for old fashioned teaching techniques and methods almost got me thrown out during my first year of medical school.

In a bacteriology course I had to learn about Tsutsugamushi fever or scrub typhus, borne by ticks, mites, fleas, or lice. First detected in Japan in 1930, it tends to be confined to a 'triangle' bound by Australia, Japan, Siberia, Pakistan and Afghanistan. It was not a U.S. risk, not in those days when travel wasn't as common now.

My bacteriology professor was the brilliant Dr. Thomas Magill. He gave pop quizzes twice a week. In the middle of something important, he'd stop the class, hand out paper, and give us an exam on anything we had covered up to that point. For example, he would ask, "How many bacteria were in the syringe that was used to inject this immunity product?"

Because of my memory I remembered what was labeled on the bottle. I whispered too loudly to my lab partner, Richard, "What a bunch of bullshit." A tap on my shoulder followed that foolish stage whisper. Standing right behind me was Professor Magill. I panicked.

"In my office," he ordered.

I waited for him a long time and when he arrived he said, "You don't like my class very much, do you?"

"Are you kidding me?" I said, hoping he wouldn't throw me out of school. "I love your course. I think it's the best course I've ever taken in my life."

"You really don't want to stay in this medical school, do you?" he said.

I was in a cold sweat. He said, "I'll tell you what. You will not take another one of my exams for the rest of the year."

"I love your exams," I gushed. "I really want to take your exams. Please allow me to take your exams."

He said, "When I call for exams, here's what I expect you to do: I expect you to stand up without one word to anyone and leave the room till the exam is over. I'm going to watch you in the next few days," he continued. "I want you to pick out several research subjects and I will choose one from among those you select, and you will write a paper on that topic."

"Okay."

"I will grade your paper," he said, "and that grade, together with the final exam, will be your grade for the course. But, for the rest of the year you won't have to take any of my other exams. Now get out of here."

The topic he selected for my paper was, "Anti-Bodies as Anti-Hormones." The theory was to take a piece of cancerous tumor from a patient, nurture it in an animal host (e.g. a mouse or a horse) so the animal develops immunity to that piece of tissue, then take the serum from the animal and separate out the immune product of that particular foreign body. It would then be injected into a patient with that same type of cancer to hopefully kill the cancer.

I started research and I spent more time on that paper, than all the studying I did for all the other courses combined. After doing this research for an entire year, I came to the conclusion that it couldn't be done because only porcelain filters would be fine enough to separate the chemical products. There were no porcelain filters of this type available yet. While the theory was sound, the technology for its practical application was not yet available. After I handed in my paper, my professor said to me, "You did a great job, but you know I can't give you an A because of what happened." So I got a B and the professor published the paper in a peer-reviewed journal with our names as co-authors.

And then many years later while watching television I heard about a scientist winning the Nobel Prize in chemistry for determining that you *can* do exactly what my paper had suggested. By then the proper filtration techniques were available. I was so angry; I sat up in bed and started screaming at the TV.

"That's mine," I yelled. I later learned his concept was similar, though with far more intricacy than I imagined.

Dr. Magill was important to my career. He taught me how to analyze problems, gather data and observations, develop concepts, formulate and express ideas and to do the hard work of research. I was convinced that Dr. Magill would have me thrown out of medical school if I hadn't. Over the years I've done a lot of research for different reasons, and the techniques and life lessons I learned from him remain important.

During the first year of medical school I decided that I would become a general practitioner, which today is known as family practice. In this field I knew I would do surgery, even though I'm not a surgeon. I would do obstetrics, even though I'm not an obstetrician, and I'd become a diagnostician, even though I wasn't an internist.

I also felt I could learn a lot more about medicine by spending time with real doctors than in some of the esoteric academic classes. So I would skip class, put on my white coat, cross the street to Kings County Hospital, and persuade a doctor into letting me walk around with him. I picked out the best teachers with the keenest minds and glued myself to them. I watched and emulated, and improvised on their concepts, ideas, techniques, and best mannerisms. I ignored those doctors who seemed perfunctory or ill-tempered.

I'd say to one of the doctors I'd targeted, "I want to walk around with you and see what you're doing."

"Where are you supposed to be?" the doctor would ask.

"I don't have class right now."

If the doctor was at heart a teacher, he would be flattered and give extra explanations while I accompanied him. One-on-one teaching is always the most productive for the medical student. My "secret" was to ask thoughtful, probing questions, listen to them, believe them, question them again, and tell them how much I appreciated their time. If you trust yourself and you can trust your doctor-mentor, and you're honest with each other, you can develop a highly effectively learning relationship.

And so with the help of these doctors I learned to do many procedures long before the medical school schedule said I was ready. These doctors also became my friends because they had found someone who wanted to emulate them. What greater compliment can you give somebody than to demonstrate that you want to learn from them? Over the years to come, I too, took on the role of mentor with anyone who wanted to learn.

In addition to "shadowing" those whom I respected, I did whatever else I needed to do to become a skilled and effective clinician. I learned various techniques for how to use the stethoscope. I learned how to understand blood pressures. By the time I finished my second year in medical school, I had already examined three hundred patients. That does not usually happen until the end of the fourth year.

Keep asking

Once when I was a third-year medical student on duty in obstetrics a 16-year-old girl was coming up the elevator with me, screaming. She was about to have a baby. I tried to calm her.

"It'll soon be over. You're having a baby, and the baby will be out soon. It'll be wonderful," I said.

"I can't be having a baby," she said angrily. "I didn't even enjoy doing it."

One secret of succeeding in medical school is to do what needs to be done, and to ask questions. Don't try to look smart, keep asking until you understand. Do not accept the first answer as infallible. If an answer is not forthcoming, ask again, check it out with someone else if time permits, look for a different avenue of thought, and don't be intimidated by error or misjudgments. Sometimes you need to ask the same question many times.

Another technique was to volunteer in an area where I could learn something new. I asked for help from those I wished to emulate and I discovered that the benefits from doing that were remarkable. I was always pushing to do procedures that a med student doesn't usually do until much later. By my third year of medical school I felt I was ready to operate on patients. I needed to figure out how to get the doctors to let me do it. I decided that doing favors for surgeons was the way to go.

I was in school in the mid-1950s when there were no mechanized laboratories. The doctors, the interns, and the students did lab work. You had to learn to do simple tests like white cell counts, blood counts, and blood-sugar urinalysis. I would stay late and volunteer to do the lab work that they hated. The surgeons thought it was great and during the day I would watch the doctors at work on their patients. After a while I said to one surgeon, "How about letting me do the next procedure?"

"Are you kidding?" he said, "You're only a third-year medical student."

"Yeah," I said, "but I have good hands and I would like to do it."

"Absolutely not."

I played my trump card. "Then I guess I won't have much time for the lab work I do for you every evening," I said. He thought about that and then said, "Well, maybe I can show you." And he showed me. The next day a patient presented with a ruptured gastric ulcer that needed immediate surgery. It was ten minutes to five in the evening, and the doctor was scheduled to go home at five. I was the one who checked the patient in. He had not seen the patient yet. It was going to take an hour to prepare the patient for surgery and so the doctor went home. I finished preparing the patient for surgery and when he was ready, I called the doctor and said, "We have a veteran here with a ruptured gastric ulcer."

"Oh really," the doctor said, "How do you know?"

I told him the tests I did, the results, the patient's physical findings, and what the X-ray showed. "You did all that?" the doctor said. "I'll be right in."

"Why don't you let me do it," I said.

"Have you done one before?" he asked.

"No," I said, "but it's like another procedure I've already done."

"I can't let you do that," he said.

"Yes, you can," I said. "If you stay near the phone. You're only a few minutes away, and if there's any problem, I'll have the nurse call you and you can drive right over. We'll keep you informed on the phone."

He said okay.

I called Rhea at home. "I'll be coming home late tonight," I said, "I'm repairing a gastric ulcer and I'm going to stay with the patient after I do it."

"You're going to do what?" she said.

I told her again.

"Who's going to be there with you?" she asked.

"I'm going to do it alone," I said. "I told the doctor. He's going to be near the phone."

I performed the operation and the patient did fine. I gained even more self-confidence and for the next six months that doctor taught me a great deal. He let me operate on other patients because he felt confident that I had the ability.

Medical students study obstetrics – delivering babies - in their fourth year, another arbitrary rule that made no sense to me. During my third year I'd go into the operating room and watch. I would go up to the doctor in charge and say, "Would you please show me how to do this?"

"You're not a fourth year student yet," he'd say, "You have to wait."

I persisted with a smile, "I have all this free time. I hate to waste it. You have a technique other doctors don't use, and I would like to watch and learn from you."

Flattered, the doctor would allow me to watch.

And then I would go to the next operating room, and say to that doctor, "Oh, you're using forceps differently than what I saw in the other room. Please show me how to do it your way." So I would be showed and I began doing deliveries at the end of my third year that other interns weren't doing until two years later. By the end of my third year, I was an experienced and dedicated student of obstetrics. I received a letter that said, "You have been awarded Student of the Year Award in Obstetrics. Would you like to have a fellowship for the summer working with Leon Chesley?"

This involved a clerkship at the significant sum, then, of $400 a month with the man who was the world's guru on toxemia pregnancy, preeclampsia, a disease that affects a substantial percent of women giving birth. Patients may have blurred vision, shortness of breath, and high blood pressure, and if not treated can suffer liver or renal failure, seizures, or have serious heart problems. Their babies are damaged or die." I certainly would," I said. I was exultant.

It was at this point I discovered that not everybody appreciated my desire to learn. I learned that some interns and residents deeply resented what I had been doing. I didn't think that anyone had paid any attention to me as I strove for a better medical education. At the end of the semester I got my med school grades. I had four A's, and a C in obstetrics.

"That can't be right," I told myself.

I went to Dr. Louis Hellman, the head of the obstetrics department. All the professors referred to him as "The Boss."

"May I talk to you, sir?" I said.

"Yes."

I showed him my grades.

"Would you take a look at this please? You see the C in obstetrics?"

"Yeah."

"I got a fellowship for being the best obstetrics student in the class."

"Yes, you did," he said.

"Do I still have my fellowship?" I asked.

"Yes, you do."

"So this C is a mistake, right? You're going to change this C, right?"

"No, I'm not," he said. "The residents are angry at you, so I won't change it. You're too aggressive. The interns and residents don't like you because they found out you were doing obstetrics far above your grade level. They had to wait and they want everyone else to wait until it comes time to learn the procedure. And I need them, because they are assistant teachers while they study. So I had to compromise the grade I wanted to give you, with what they wanted to give you, which was a D or F, so you got a C. Have a nice day."

This happened in 1956. Dr. Hellman taught me that how others viewed me was important. Humility trumps arrogance. It would play an important role in my life again and again. For example, when I was in my second year of medical school, I was doing some third-year work. I was leaning how to conduct internal examinations on women. I was about to do an exam of a woman in her 80s. Women at that age are very sensitive and very particular about exposure. It can be very painful for them to have a vaginal examination because of their age and because their tissues have thinned.

I was using the smallest of all instruments, and I was going to be very careful. She was cooperative. She was in stirrups and after a few minutes she raised her head and looked at me through her knees, and said with a smile, "Does your mother know what you are doing?

She was trying to be funny, but in her way, she was saying, "You're much too young to be here between my legs. You are much too young to have anything to do with this part of my anatomy."

She decided she was going to make friends with me instead of teaching me a lesson. I learned to pay attention to how an older person is treated and how she reacts. I learned that an older person has different thought processes and recognizes gentleness more than a younger person. In other words, if you take an older person by the hand, it tells them, I care about you. If you take a younger woman by the hand, she thinks you're flirting with her. The intention might be the same, but it will be interpreted differently.

Cheating

Cheating takes different forms and is not always equated with dishonesty. I was assigned for three months to evaluate newborn infants and to write reports of the worst genetic abnormalities. The parents didn't want these infants or were unable to care for them, so they were placed in a part of the hospital where they were nurtured and studied. They were physically deformed and mentally disabled and usually died within two or three months. It was such a horrible experience for me that I could not persist with this assignment. There were many interested professionals specializing in these fields, but I knew I was not suited. After doing the minimum required in this course, instead of more than needed as was my usual way, I would wander to different wards in Kings County Hospital, find a resident, and say, "Can I hang out here for a couple of hours. I'd like to watch and learn from you."

The interns would almost always say, "Yes, sure."

After about three hours I would go back and check the records of the disabled infants and write my reports from those records instead of from a personal examination of the children. I learnt something from these babies; that professionals can and do write entries in records that are not always related to what really happened. Doctors write things they don't hear or didn't see. They will write about an examination that they didn't do. They make comments in a lab report that cannot possibly be true because they probably never looked in on the patient. As a lawyer and medical records evaluator in the years to come, I can attest that sometimes a doctor might write something in the record for a day when they were off. Six months later somebody will look at the report and say, "Pretty good." Thirty years later the shortcuts I learned in this rotation helped me a lot in malpractice case understanding and evaluation.

CHAPTER 6

KINGS COUNTY

Everyone who came into the Kings County Hospital Emergency Room was poor, badly injured, medically disenfranchised, or all three. If you didn't have the money to pay for a private doctor, you would go to the emergency room. As a doctor at Kings County Hospital you could learn more in one year than in almost any other hospital in the United States. There were only three or four hospitals like it in the country, one was in New Orleans, another in Chicago, and one in Boston. All the immigrants, the farmers, the poorly educated, the unemployed, the criminals, the mentally ill, and those who didn't go to a doctor until they had five illnesses at one time, would show up in the emergency room. It was a museum of pathology.

On a Saturday night you could see five gunshot wounds on different people, gunshot and knife wounds on the same person, people whose liver was damaged, others dying of heart disease because they were diabetic, and alcoholics stricken with disease. There were patients in car accidents with multiple fractures and internal injuries. Women came in with botched abortions, some had been raped and who had broken bones. And then there were the malingerers.

One woman was about 60-years-old. The doctors had no idea what was wrong with her, so they admitted her to the hospital. At that time, once you were admitted, you could not be sent home unless there was someone to take you, this meant some people who no longer needed hospital care were in the hospital for weeks.

She was first put in a room for four patients, but she was such a miserable person, the ward administrators put her in a room with two beds. Then they put her in a private room. Nobody wanted to room with her. No one wanted to care for her.

The only time anyone was forced to see her was during the Saturday grand rounds. The chairman of the department would lead medical students around, teaching and orally testing students in diagnostics. He would ask difficult questions, the purpose of which was to make you think and feel like you didn't know very much. The chief was in front, the chief resident behind him, and the third-year residents were behind them. The poor medical students were way in the back. Every year you moved closer to the front.

This woman was insufferable. The hospital staff tried to transfer her to different departments, but everyone would consult and they would refuse to take her because she was so difficult. She didn't really have what she complained about or thought she had. She just wanted to be in the hospital. One night about two o'clock in the morning one of the interns hatched a plan to get rid of her. He came into her room, stood at the foot of her bed while she was awake and urinated all over her.

Saturday came and during the grand rounds everyone stood by her bed. When the chairman started discussing her case and asking questions, she began screaming, "There he is! There he is!"

"What are you talking about, ma'am?"

"At two in the morning he came in here and peed all over me," she said.

Everyone was sure she was crazy. They ordered an emergency transfer to the psychiatric ward.

Limited

Kings County Hospital is built over miles of underground tunnels. Once I got lost for three hours in them. The tunnels go in all different directions following the pipes and electric power lines. You can go four city blocks underground. On one end of the campus was Kings County Hospital and at the other was the Student Union Building, here the residents went to drink beer and eat pizza. There was a pool table in the lounge where nobody could bother you.

On one occasion, the then director of the hospital, a disagreeable person, called a meeting and told us that there would be strict limits on who could use what medical instruments. He wanted us to sign in when we took an instrument and sign out when we put it back. It was ridiculous. There are many times you need little instruments: clips to tie rubber bands around when you take blood and small suture scissors to remove stitches. You use an instrument and habitually you put it in your pocket to use when you need it again. Now we would have to account for every little instrument. It was a waste of time that could be devoted to patient care.

One morning the operating room staff came in to discover that one of the eight operating room tables was missing. They couldn't find it. Everyone was upset. One of the chief residents invited the director of the hospital through a long tunnel over to the student lounge and there was the missing operating table.

The staff told the hospital director, "We work hard, and once in a while we do take a pair of scissors or something to use on your patients, our concern is the patient and so we don't always remember to put the scissors back. You're worried about scissors? Well, we just stole an operating table. We'll bring it back but you'd better get rid of that rule about having to sign out small instruments or other things will disappear." He rescinded the rule.

CHAPTER 7

THE KING OF SAND HILL

Dr. Perrin Long was the chairman of the Department of Internal Medicine at Kings County. During the Second World War he achieved the rank of General. He was the toughest, meanest, and most unapproachable of all the professionals in the college. But I never skipped one of his classes. When he taught internal diagnostics every word was a pearl of wisdom. If you missed one class, you missed an entire chapter. Influenced by him and my dad's experience, when I was in my fourth year of medical school, I applied to join the Army.

My paperwork was complete but I had not yet been called for my physical. There were only three days left until the end of the application process. Once the three days were up, I would lose my opportunity to enlist for the coming year.

I went to Dr. Long's office and said I wanted to join the Army but I hadn't yet been called for my physical. "Let me tell you about the Army, son," said the former General. "After my thirty-two years in the Army, I had my future in front of me. Why don't you wait? Finish your residency first. Then if you still want to go into the Army, you can."

"No," I said, "I want to go into the Army now."

"Okay, just a minute," he said, and picked up the phone. He called First Army Headquarters, which was on Governor's Island near the Statue of Liberty. He asked to speak with the medical officer who was in charge of the physicals for applicants.

"Is this Captain Butler? I don't know you, but this is General Long. I wonder if you could do me a big favor. I have a medical student sitting with me who has applied for the Army, but he hasn't yet heard about his physical. His time is up in three days, and I wonder if you could expedite that? I would really appreciate it. What did you say your name was? Captain Butler."

He looked at me and said, "Harry, when can you go down there?"

"I can go at any time," I said.

"He says he can go at any time. Yes, he can be there this afternoon."

He hung up, and he said, "Look for Captain Butler, and they'll do your physical today." Then he said to me, "Did you hear that conversation?"

"Yes, sir," I said.

"I never call myself General Long," he said. "I'm Dr. Long. I haven't been a general in a long time, but sometimes you have to gently use power, and make sure the person that you're using it with knows that you know his name, and that you will remember it."

I went and took my physical, which took no more than five minutes. Captain Butler said, "Why don't I interview you while you're still here?"

I was accepted into the Army, where I would spend the best three years of my professional life.

When I first entered the army at Fort Benning, Georgia, I was assigned to care for the recruits in training at Sand Hill. I was assigned to a building not much bigger than the living room of my modest house, it had two rooms, one bigger and one smaller. It had no air-conditioning, no phone, and almost no equipment. Essentially, it was a screening area for the sick. If a recruit needed something more than an aspirin, or mustard plaster, or an enema, you sent him to the hospital for an evaluation.

I was on duty from seven in the morning until five in the afternoon, and I would have thirty-five or forty recruits lined up for sick call. I was a filter. They either got pills or were sent to the hospital. It didn't take me long to figure out I wouldn't do very much after the initial sick call. Within the first week I found myself bored to tears.

I was assigned to the Army hospital and one day, while walking around and getting to know the place, I ended up in the dermatology clinic. A group of Army doctors were trying to diagnose a patient who had an unusual rash on her hands. The head doctor was asking, "What do you think it is? What do you think we ought to do?" He went around to each doctor except me, so I commented, "You might consider leprosy." Her hands looked like those of a patient I had seen two and a half years earlier at Kings County.

The other doctors looked at me as if to say, "Who are you? What do you know?"

Later the chief, who was a Lieutenant Colonel, called me over and said, "The other doctors told me what you did. Who do you think you are? Don't do that again."

"Yes, sir," I said.

A week later the chief called me on the phone.

"Your attitude wasn't appreciated," he said, "but it was leprosy. How did you know?"

I told him. I had come out of Kings County Hospital, the Mecca of medical knowledge, where you see more on a Saturday night than a year in a small community hospital. Even though I worked in the Fort Benning emergency room, not very much happened. Someone might have a sprained knee, or a sore throat, or a splinter in his butt.

One day I told an intern partner.

"This is the most boring job; I don't know why I came here."

The screen opened up behind me, and in strode a major in the Medical Corps who had overheard me. He dismissed everyone else and sat me down.

He asked me where I came from and said, "You will never practice medicine again like you did at Kings County hospital. That was a great learning experience, but in private practice you need to learn from every patient that you meet. That will make it an easier job, and if you focus on learning from every patient, you will never have that feeling of boredom and frustration that you have just expressed."

That major taught me something that I think about daily. There are days when you wonder, "Why am I here and what am I doing? I cannot wait for this day to be over." Whenever that happens, the memory of the major appears before me.

Once I ran into a homeless person on the street in Washington DC. He wouldn't let go of me. And then I thought of the major, and I started having a conversation with him. When we left the conversation ten minutes later, we were both better people. I have been fortunate at every critical point in my life or career to have met special people who said something meaningful to me and pointed the way.

One day a major came to me with a hemorrhoid thrombosis. It is agony. You relieve it by cutting it open and removing the clot, which in turn out relieves the pressure that causes the pain. You can do it by using a local anesthesia. If you do it right, you become the patient's best friend.

I'd first performed it on my father in my third year of medicine. He was in agony and after five minutes, I had relieved him of his pain.

"My son with the golden hands," proclaimed my mother.

I figured if I could do it in the bathroom at home, I could do it anyplace. I told the major, "I can send you to the hospital or I can fix it."

"Will it hurt?" he asked.

"Yes," I said.

"Okay, do it," he ordered.

When I checked back with him the next morning I asked him how he felt.

"I'm fine," he said. "Amazing, how did you do it?"

It was at that point that he became my friend, and heaven knows, I needed him to be my friend to improve the barren Sand Hill clinic.

"Major," I said, "I need your help. It's July. It's 96 degrees. This place is not air-conditioned. I only have window fans. There's no phone, and I have no room to work. Would you help me a little?"

The next morning when I arrived I saw I had a window air conditioner, two telephone lines, and some equipment that hadn't been there before. Within three months I converted that space into a mini-operating room, and I was doing the kind of procedures I was trained for that didn't require me to send patients to the hospital.

Not only did the major and his wife become my patients, but the base colonel and his wife, and the lieutenant-colonel and his wife as well. Anytime I needed anything to improve the clinic's quality, I got it. My clinic became a mini-outpatient center.

For the next three years I became the King of Sand Hill. For two or three hours every morning, I ran my own hospital. The sergeant who worked with me was a veteran and a great marksman. He helped with everything I needed. We had a great relationship. He lent me his Jeep and saw to it that I had a helicopter and pilot when I needed it. He taught me how to use his marksman pistol and he kept me from freezing to death.

Every winter we had to spend two weeks in tank training at Fort Stewart, Georgia. Part of training required sleeping in a tent in January, even if it was snowing. I was medical doctor for the tank battalion. Everyone was supposed to pile into jeeps and ride as a unit. I took my car. When I arrived, I went to the dispensary, which turned out to be a large room with some equipment in it, but that was it. It was set up once a year for this purpose.

"That's your tent out there," I was told. "There's a major and two other officers in there with you. You'll be fine."

I said to my sergeant, "I'm not going to do that."

"You have to," he said.

"No," I said, "I can't sleep in a tent. My mother didn't raise me to sleep in a tent."

I walked around the dispensary and I noticed it had a closet about five feet wide and about eight feet long.

"How about if I sleep in the closet?" I said. "I take this bench and put it in there. There's a coal fire in the building, I'll be warm."

"Well," my sergeant said, "there is inspection in the morning at about six o'clock."

"Just lock me in," I said. "There's a padlock on the door. It's a storage closet. If someone says, 'Open the closet,' just say that Dr. Rein has the key, and that he's out and not back yet."

And so I slept in that the closet each night for two weeks. Sure enough there was a general inspection and the inspector asked, "Where's the key?"

My sergeant said, "Dr. Rein has it, but he's not here yet."

The inspector left. My sergeant unlocked the door and I emerged after a good night's sleep. I slept warm the whole time.

Thanks to my sergeant, I learned to drive a tank, to fire a weapon, and how to best help injured soldiers. The Army is an exaggeration of real life. It prepares you to work with all kinds of different personalities. You learn to take orders and you learn to give orders; if you do it by encouraging people rather than pushing them around, you get good results.

In the Army you learn to question authority rather than challenge it. I never did learn to do that very well. I challenged authority for the first twenty years of my professional life, and many times that caused ill will toward me. I was accused of being pushy and trying to do too much too fast. Maybe, but I also think many doctors are jealous of their own positions and that makes some insecure.

In the Army I also learned if you ask, "How should I do that?" and "Would you teach me how..." you get a better result.

I try to teach young professionals and students that knowing what you don't know is as important as what you understand. Never fear asking "How?"

The Army is a corporation. A huge corporation. It's an opportunity to maximize what's available and take advantage of a learning process. Vacuum information from those who are willing to give it to you. Be prepared to offer help with what they need.

Whenever I disagreed with a superior officer in the Army I quickly learned that saying something like, "If I did it differently, would it help you more?" took the sting out of what might be considered criticism.

Managing ego is important in the Army. Those who think, "I'm the most important person around me," are lonely. A multimillionaire may have an entourage, but when the money dries up, that entourage disappears very quickly. And so there are generals, and colonels, and majors in the Army, and chiefs of departments in hospitals who have people following them around to boost their ego. Until they realize that they can't function without those people around them. When a person recognizes that, his life gets better.

In the army I maximized opportunities. I didn't do anything great. I just wanted to learn. In the army, as in every profession, there are great opportunities to slack off because there are so many people around doing the same job.

The single most important happening in my army career came early. I had just been promoted to captain. I really didn't know how to wear the uniform properly, but it didn't matter because as soon as you go to work, you open your tie, take off your jacket, and roll up your sleeves.

I was supposed to run my clinic all day, but I only ran it from 7am to 8:30am, and then I would drive to the hospital. I knew that in three years I would be starting my own medical practice and I wanted to be prepared. And so I showed up at the hospital every day – I was a captain and I wore a white coat with a medical insignia - and in the same way that I'd learned a lot during my medical training, I would ask one of the doctors, "I would like to assist you and learn your techniques."

They always said yes.

One of my duties was to learn to give anesthesia to patients before an operation. Ether was still used. It took 45 minutes for someone to get anesthetized enough to withstand surgery. Today we have Propofol, the drug that killed Michael Jackson. Propofol takes between twenty seconds and a minute and a half to work its magic so the surgeon can get to work.

I was giving ether to a soldier who was going to have a toe amputated, when I noticed that the doctor doing the surgery was cleaning the toe on the opposite foot. I was reluctant to say something because he was my superior and with nurses around us, I didn't want to show him up. I also didn't want him cutting off the soldier's good toe.

"Colonel," I said, "have you checked the record in this case?"

He brushed me off.

"Just tell me when you're ready with the anesthetic," he said.

He was scrubbing and cleaning, and he was putting the dressings on, pre-op, and I made three or four hints that should have made him realize he was about to operate on the guy's wrong foot. He didn't get the hint, so just before the patient went under, I had no choice but to say in a voice loud enough for everyone to hear, "Sir, you're cutting on the wrong foot."

He looked me up and down with scorn, then realized that what I was saying was true, so he switched to the correct foot and cleaned it in preparation for surgery. He finished cleaning and did the surgery.

The next day he pulled me aside and reamed me out for making him look bad in front of the nurses.

"I tried to tell you four different ways," I said. "I asked you to please look at the chart, to see if the toe was any better or worse before you went into surgery. You ignored me. And when you were about to cut, I didn't know what else to say."

"You made it very obvious to everyone in the operating room that you think I'm an idiot," he said.

"No, sir," I said. "I don't think you're an idiot, you're five ranks above me and I was as polite as I could be."

The colonel never spoke to me ever again.

One of the things I am proudest of about my army service was changing the way soldiers getting out of the army with disabilities were treated. It began when one day a 20-year old obese, clumsy private walked into my clinic. He said he had flat feet, his arm hurt, and he couldn't sleep. I checked him out. He seemed fine. He came back. I checked him out again, and he still seemed fine. When he came back the third, fourth, and fifth times, I felt certain he was a malingerer.

"Get out of here," I told him, "Go back to work."

Around the same time, I ran into a doctor radiologist who had served in the army ten years after his residency. He was being discharged. He had just returned from his discharge physical, and someone noted he had a rhythm abnormality in his heart. I noted in the discharge rules and regulations that if the arrhythmia begins in the army, it's a service-related issue, and he's entitled to disability. A disability at that time was the percent of your salary on which you paid no taxes, it also created an entitlement to treatment for the arrhythmia for the rest of his life.

I told him that.

"The rules don't provide for it."

"Yes, they do." And I showed him the book.

"Thank you, Harry," he said.

I realized that a lot of people were getting discharged with disabilities that they didn't have. One day I was summoned by the commanding officer of Sand Hill.

"We have a complaint," he said.

The complaint was by the malingerer. He was the son of a congressman and his complaint was that I would not discharge him with a disability. I gave the commanding officer my impressions and added,

"Why don't you send him out of the army? He doesn't belong here anyway. He doesn't fit the medical qualifications."

"Do it for me, would you?" he said.

"I can't," I said. "He doesn't meet the medical qualifications, but if you give me a direct order, Colonel, then I'll do it."

"I can't order you to do it if it's a medical issue," he said.

"If you can't order me to do it," I said, "I can't do it."

Two days later I was ordered to report to the commander of Fort Benning. I walked in and saluted rather casually. The general said, "Do you always salute that way, Captain?"

As I stood at attention, the general said, "I understand you won't discharge Private So-and-so."

"That's right, sir."

The general told me the congressman wanted his son discharged because the kid was sending letters home about how unhappy he was. "It would be better for the army if we discharged him," said the general, "because this representative might visit Fort Benning and cause me all sorts of headaches. Why don't you just go ahead and discharge him?"

"As soon as you order me to do that, I will, sir," I said.

"I can't order you to," the general said. "You're the doctor in charge of Sand Hill."

"Well," I said, "he doesn't meet the medical qualifications."

"You don't like the army very much, do you, Captain?" he said.

"I like the army, sir, but there are many problems with the disability program. I just met a doctor who is being discharged without a disability even though he has one. Now you want me to discharge a man with disability when he doesn't have one. The system is broken."

"I suppose you can fix it," the general said.

"Yes," I said. "I think I can."

"How much time do you need?"

"I'll need at least four months."

"Do it. You're dismissed."

"Sir, may I have written orders because to go to the hospital and inquire in different departments and make suggestions... I know if they see this young captain coming, they won't pay me any attention. But if I have orders from you to evaluate the disability system and make suggestions then I can be of service."

"Write an order," he said, "and I'll sign it."

I wrote one that allowed me entry into every department of the hospital and to evaluate consultations. He signed it. I showed the order to the hospital's commanding general, who didn't like the idea.

"Sir," I said, "It will not affect you at all. I will not be intrusive. If my observations can improve this system, it will be good for everybody in the service."

"Well, go ahead."

I went from department to department, showing my orders to the chief of each. I learned the ins and outs of all the medical departments. I even assisted in surgery. I attached myself to Yale Zimberg, a surgeon with great hands, and he taught me how to do appendectomies, gastric ulcers, hernia repairs, and hemorrhoid surgery. I must have performed three hundred operations, including two hundred major operations.

My wife was supportive when I stayed away from home every other night for almost three years to get this training.

The changes I made meant that if someone had a heart rhythm abnormality, they needed to see a cardiologist instead of being discharged just by anybody. If they had an ankle problem, they had to be seen by an orthopedist. And so on.

Teaching

I was once woken by the phone at about three in the morning, Joe Cataldo, a first lieutenant and an intern, was on the phone.

"One of your patients was injured and has a lung full of blood," Joe said.

"How do you know?" I asked.

"I took an x-ray," he said.

"What do you think?" I asked.

"I think it needs to be drained," he said.

"I think you're right," I said. "Do it."

"I have never done that before," he said.

"Well, you're going to do it right now," I told him.

"How?"

"Here's the set up. It will take you ten minutes to get it ready," I told him. "Get a nurse, and you'll have me on the phone. The nurse will hold it to your ear and I'll walk you through it."

I walked Joe through the procedure. He drained a pint and a half of blood out of the patient's lung, despite never having done it before.

"Everything looks good," Joe said. "I'll call you if I need you. Thank you very much."

I hung up, went back to sleep, and the next morning arrived at the hospital. I got into the elevator, and when I got out, I saw Joe, and he said, "The patient is doing fine."

"Really?" I said. "Which patient?"

"Sergeant Burns, sir," he said.

"Who is Sergeant Burns?"

"He was the patient with the lung I drained last night," he said. "You walked me through it, and I appreciate that."

I had no memory of doing it. When people say they can do something in their sleep, it's true.

With six months remaining of my tour, my sergeant and I decided to properly equip the clinic. I made a list of what we needed: dressings, clips, bandages, and small hand instruments.

About a week before I left for Orlando to go into private practice, he pulled up in a Jeep. He had two huge trunks in the back and brought one of them into the clinic

"Here," he said. "Here's all the stuff you're going to need for the clinic."

It was perfect; everything I would have wanted and other things he thought would help stock the place. After we finished distributing it all, he said to me, "Come on out to the jeep."

In the back of the jeep was a second trunk, identical to the first one.

"What do you have in there?" I asked.

"The exact same thing," he said.

"But we don't need any more equipment," I said.

"It's a going-away present for you," he said.

He gave me supplies that would last a year for my general practice office. Inside the trunk were stethoscopes, specula and other instruments, hundreds of bandages, an otoscope, and an ophthalmoscope. "I thought you would like this, and it would make life easier for you, just like you've made life easier for us here," he said.

Family medicine

Near the time of my discharge in 1960, the American Board of Family Practice was created. There had been boards in other specialties, but not in family medicine, now there was a residency program and a first exam. I was allowed to take the exam while I was still in the army.

The board examinations were over three days: two days of written exams and a day of oral examination at Grady Memorial Hospital in Atlanta, Georgia, a huge charity hospital similar to Kings County Hospital in Brooklyn.

Part of the exam entailed me doing a complete physical examination of a patient, taking a history, and making an evaluation. I was given as long as I wanted and then I was to be questioned about the patient for an hour.

I had spent almost two and a half years in the Army, running my own clinic and I felt I knew everything necessary to pass the exam. Now I know that every day brings a new learning experience.

The woman patient I was to evaluate was in her late 70s, perhaps early 80s. I was in the midst of examining her when she said, "Please be gentle. You people taking the exam have examined me eight times today. I have a small tumor on my thyroid gland and you can't feel it unless you press really hard on my neck and when you do, it hurts. They told me it was benign, so I don't have to worry about it."

She had given me the diagnosis.

I was gentle as I felt it, though I might not have found the tumor had she not told me about it. During my oral exam, my professor and I discussed my diagnosis. I said,

"I really don't know for sure what she has, but maybe she has a tumor in her thyroid gland."

There was silence.

"How did you come up with that?"

"Well," I said, "it was pretty obvious that she has a thyroid problem but the cause is a mystery. The way I came up with that was exclusion." I couldn't be dishonest. "Well, actually, the way I came up with that is," I said sheepishly, "she told me."

My professor paused and then smiled.

"You know you were set up, don't you?" he said.

"What do you mean?"

"She told each of you taking the exam what she had. We told her what to say, and you were the only one to admit that she had told you."

"I've been in the service and I've seen so many bad things happen," I said. "When you lie, life becomes very complicated. You have to remember the lies. Life is easier if you tell the truth." I passed and became one of the first family practice specialists in the United States.

CHAPTER 8

MAGICAL FLORIDA

During the last year of military service, whenever there was an opportunity Rhea and I would drive six to eight hours from Fort Benning, Georgia down to Orlando and look around. The Eisenhower highway system had not yet been built. We drove highway 441 and 301, two-lane roads all the way.

After my discharge from the U.S. Army, Rhea and I, with our daughters Robin, three-years-old, and Debra, one-year-old, moved to Orlando. I'd waited a decade to live in the city of my dreams. I fell in love with Orlando after my first year at NYU, it was July 1951. I had a few dollars in my pocket and I decided to take a trip to Miami, on my way I stopped in the little town of Orlando, because my mother's sister, "Tante Anny," lived there. Anny was one of my favorite aunts, but it had been years since I had last seen her.

She was glad to see me and suggested I stay for a few days. I spent time with sons of her friends who were also home from college and were hanging out for the summer in Orlando. There were four of them and we went swimming in the local pool and to bars. They had money, a car, beer, girls and friends – I never got to Miami. I stayed with my aunt and my new friends for the full ten days and found a new world.

One of those attending the University of Florida lived on a farm. He had a swimming pool and a big, black four-door Buick that went 90 miles an hour. In the evenings we drove to Gainesville, an hour and a half away by car. We drank beer and made noise with the University of Florida girls as the jukebox was playing. We played a lot of pool, it was so much fun. These were warm, friendly people. Most of the time we spent swimming, hanging around, and playing pool. These people are still my friends today. It's why, when I returned to New York, I promised myself, "When I finish my medical training, I'm going to open a practice in Orlando."

As a New Yorker, Florida with its orange trees, many lakes, water skiing, alligators, and beaches seemed magical. When I was between the third and fourth year of medical school, my wife and I drove to Miami for a vacation. It was the summer of 1956. I had a car, a yellow, two-door DeSoto. You'd put it in third gear and drive without shifting. We had a reservation at the Empress Motel in Miami Beach. We were going to splurge and stay in one of the expensive rooms, which were $32 a night. It was a luxurious vacation for less than $500.

We left New York and as I drove through Fayetteville, North Carolina, a flashing light went on behind me.

"Where are you going, buddy?" I was asked by a local policeman.

"I'm going to Florida," I said.

"Well, you're going pretty fast," he said. "Come with me."

"I wasn't going that fast," I tried to argue.

"You understand me, boy?" he said. "Follow me."

We arrived at a one-room combination police station, courthouse, and jail. I walked in, and there were two cells. One of them was empty. The other held an African-American prisoner. Sitting there was a sheriff and a couple of deputies.

"Man," the cop said, "you were speeding, and you're going to go before the judge."

"I'm sorry," I said indignantly, "but I wasn't speeding."

"If you want to contest this," the cop said, "we can have a trial. You can tell it to the judge. Today is Thursday, and he'll be here on Tuesday."

"I can't do that," I said. "I'm a medical student. I'm on vacation. My wife is in the car."

"If you want to contest it, you can do just as this fellow over here is doing," he said. He was referring to the man in the cell.

"May I just pay my fine and go?" I asked contritely.

"You want to pay your fine?" he said. "It'll be $35," which was a lot of money back then for a speeding ticket.

"How much?" I howled.

"Do you have trouble hearing, boy?" he said.

"No, sir," I said.

I took out thirty-five dollars, thinking to myself, there goes money for a whole night's hotel stay, and I handed it to him.

"Now get on your way," the cop said.

"May I please have a receipt?" I asked him.

He looked at me like I was a moron. He took out what looked like a dime store pad, and on the top of one of the pages he wrote the number 35 and a dollar sign. He handed it to me, and he said, "I think that'll do. Do you understand me?"

"Yes, sir," I said.

I got into my car and drove away. For the next twenty miles a police car followed us. It was a horrible experience.

CHAPTER 9

ESTABLISHING MY PRACTICE

When my wife and I came to Orlando for one of our visits in March 1960, I suggested, "You look for a house that you might be interested in buying. Here's our budget. I'm going to look for an office." We found what we were looking for on opposite ends of Orlando.

I rented a storefront in a strip mall. It was an empty shell, so I had to remodel. I estimated it would cost me about $6,000 to remodel the space and add some furniture to make it look like a doctor's office. I had never borrowed money before, but was told that I, as a professional, needed to establish credit.

I found two branches of the same bank which each agreed to lend me $3,000, but no more. The same bank, two branches, the same day, and neither knew about the other.

I started making payments. Three months later the bank discovered I had borrowed the $3,000 twice, and they called me.

"Didn't you know it was the same bank?" I was asked.

"One is on Orange Avenue, and one is on Edgewater Drive," I said.

"Didn't you look at the sign?"

"I went to the bank, and I borrowed the money," I said. "I don't remember."

"Nobody has ever done this to us before," I was told.

I visited the banks personally to pay off my loans. We got to like each other and soon most of the employees of the bank became my patients, as did their friends, who sent their friends, who sent relatives. And every time I went into either of the banks, they would laugh, "Here he is, this kid who comes into town and scams us, and now he's our doctor."

I made friends quickly, developed trust, and over fifty-five years built a reputation of integrity. I got lucky when the person I was buying medical equipment from said to me, "Are you looking for a nurse?"

I said I was.

"A good friend of mine is a nurse downtown," he said, "and she doesn't like her job. She's very experienced and would like to leave. She's attractive and smart, and she works hard. You'll like her. Why don't you give her a try?"

The timing was perfect. Ginger Watson became my office princess. She had about eight-years of experience. Whatever I needed with respect to compensation forms, insurance forms, billing, collections, I left up to her, because I had no idea what to do.

Of course, there are no patients until you put a sign on the door and by the window. I was a young doctor with a crewcut who looked like he had just come out of grade school. One of the first things I did was join a synagogue. I went to a service, and shook hands with everyone. I walked across the street to the Edgewater High School, and announced, "I'm Dr. Rein. I'm opening across the street. If I may be of service to you, let me know."

I opened my practice in July 1960. On the second day I was open, I looked at my calendar and there were three patients all scheduled for two o'clock in the afternoon.

I asked Ginger why she did that.

"Wouldn't we be better off if you spread them out?"

"No, no, no," she said. "Let me explain this to you: When they all come in at two, it will look like you're busy. They'll say to themselves:

"This brand new family doctor already has patients. If the office seems empty, the patients might wonder whether they made a mistake coming to you. "

So the three patients came in, and they commented out loud, "Isn't it nice that this new doctor already has patients." After they left they told their friends, "I went to Dr. Rein's office and he already has patients. He must be good. There's something about him."

What Ginger did in just my first week of practice was amazing.

At first I had very little to do so I would go around to every – and I mean every – family doctor and internal medicine clinic in Central Florida and knock on the door and introduce myself. I would say, "I'm the new kid on the block. I'm on Edgewater Drive, and on nights and weekends, and holidays this summer, if you would like to take a vacation, I will be very happy to take your calls for you. If you hire me, in the morning on your desk, there will be a note of whom I saw, what I thought the diagnosis was, and what I prescribed. I will never see any of your patients a second time, because they are your patients. But if a new patient calls you, and I get to see him, and he wants me to see him again, I will see him. But I'll never steal a patient, and I'll take calls for you." It would give them time off and allow me to practice and it worked.

A lot of doctors hired me to substitute for them on nights, weekends, during their vacations, and whenever they wanted more time with their family for summer activities. Within a month I was busy twenty-four hours a day, seven days a week with night calls and emergency room calls. That August, just two months after I started, was the busiest month of my entire fifty-five-year career. Every morning at six a.m. I would drive from hospital to hospital to visit my patients and also other doctor's patients when I was on call for them. I never went to sleep. I was up all day and made night calls, house calls and weekend calls. And it made my practice.

All the doctors were happy because I never stole their patients and word got around that you could trust Dr. Rein. One of the doctors I was working with was Dr. Thomas Heggert, the Medical Examiner of Orange County, Florida. Any time there is an unattended death, the body has to be looked at by the medical examiner who decides whether it's a homicide, suicide, or a natural death. If it's anything but a natural death, there has to be an autopsy, and the cause of death has to be explained.

Dr. Heggert asked if I would like to help him with his work as medical examiner, having subbed for him for the previous six weeks with house calls and weekend calls.

"I'm going away for a couple of weeks," he said. "How would you like to be the Acting-Medical Examiner of Orange County for a while?"

"I haven't the slightest idea what to do," I said. In two hours he gave me the essentials of what I had to do.

"When I come back," he said, "I'll pick up the pieces, and I'll write the reports."

It was exciting and opened doors to the world of forensics. I got home one night from house calls at one in the morning. The plan was to get a few hours sleep before the phone rang again.

It soon did.

"We have a death at Orange Blossom South Trail. Are you the Medical Examiner?" asked the caller.

I said I was, and asked for directions. I was new to town and had no idea where the body lay. I got in my car and started driving. I found the street. I made a left turn and headed down a hill toward a lake. I could see the blinking red lights of the fire engines, so I knew I was in the right place. There was a crowd of people.

I parked my car, picked up my black bag, and got out. I started walking, and as I got closer the crowd separated, just like in the movies. Here comes the medical examiner!

I walked toward the water and there lying on the ground was a body that had just been dragged out of the lake. It had been in the water two or three days, so it was decomposing. The skin was coming off, and it was just rotting away.

Yes, this guy is dead, all right, I thought. We're going to do an autopsy on this one for sure. I'm not going to let some guy get murdered and dumped in the lake on my watch. A sergeant from the sheriff's office was standing right next to me. He knew the medical examiner and he had never seen me before.

"Doc," he said, "is this your first one?"

"Yes," I said.

He whispered, "Well, you're supposed to pronounce him dead. We can't move the body until he's officially pronounced dead by the medical examiner."

"Yeah, okay, sure," I said.

I was thinking, "How do I do that?" I remembered in the movies how the actor playing the medical examiner would shine a light in a dead man's eyes. I never learned why. I had a light in my bag. I bent down, and I took the light out of my bag, thinking, with distaste, I have to touch this decomposing body without gloves.

I bent down. I pulled one eyelid open and shone the light like I was looking for something. It was horrible.

I stood up, put the light away, and I said out loud for all to hear, "I pronounce you dead."

Everybody started laughing. The sheriff and the firemen were laughing, and so we sent the body to the morgue for an autopsy.

I had the occasion to walk into the sheriff's office maybe thirty times for the next two years for one reason or another, and every time I would walk in, they would say, "Hi Doc, I now pronounce you dead." I laughed and they laughed, we became good friends and developed trust.

For a doctor, death is part of the job. I never liked it, but it never really interfered with me; it was a learning experience each time.

In the early years of my practice there were no answering machines, no beepers, only answering services. They could page you. I took advantage of that. I would tell the answering service, "I will be in such and such restaurant at 5:30. Would you please page Dr. Rein at 5:45?" If I went to a football game, I would have myself paged twice at the game, just to make sure my name was heard on the loudspeakers.

"Dr. Rein, emergency call for you."

People would wonder, "Who is this Dr. Rein being paged?"

Once in a while one of them at the game might think, "Maybe I'll try Dr. Rein. "And they did. Within three months I had the busiest office I could ever hope to have. Occasionally it was standing room only.

CHAPTER 10

SMILE WITH YOUR EYES

One evening after six, David, a patient who was a lawyer, and a friend, came charging into the office.

"Harry, Harry, you have to help," he said.

"I'm leaving, David," I said, "and you don't look sick."

"It's not me," he said. "It's a good friend. He's been hurt in a car accident, and he's in the hospital, I don't think he's being treated well. You have to come and see him."

"No, I'm not going to see him," I said. "I'm going home."

"You have to do me a favor," he said.

I reluctantly agreed and went to the hospital. His friend had one leg in a cast up to his hip in traction and a nasal oxygen tube. I could see that this was an orthopedic calamity. Sitting in the room was a nice-looking, youngish woman.

I examined him and found there were two or three other things wrong with him. I was sure he had a lacerated liver, which was still bleeding, his spleen was swelling, and he probably had pneumonia either from aspirating something, maybe the medication, or just from lying in bed for several days.

I went to the nurses' station to be certain the nurses and his treating orthopedists knew about these findings.

"Dr. Rein," one of the nurses said, "we are so glad you're here. We have a serious problem."

"You don't know the half of it," I said and started to describe the physical signs I found.

"No, no, that's not what I'm talking about," the nurse said. "You're going to have to get that woman out of there."

"Why?"

"Twice now, we've gone in, and she was giving him oral sex," she said.

I really didn't care about that. It was late, I needed to see the patient was treated properly and I wanted to get home, it was now after 10 pm. When I arrived home, I cleaned up and was getting ready for bed, when Rhea asked me about the patient.

"Oh some guy, he was a mess," I said.

I had not the slightest idea who he was; to me he was a badly injured patient who needed a lot of care.

"Was his name Joe Foxfire (not his real name)," she asked.

"Yes, how did you know?"

"You don't know who Joe Foxfire is, do you?" she asked.

"No."

"He's Central Florida's gambling kingpin."

"Are you kidding?" I said.

"No," she said.

"Well, I don't really want to have anything to do with him. I was involved with the Gallo gang when I was 10, and I really don't need any more of it."

I continued to take care of him, and two weeks later he was discharged. He thanked me graciously, and said, "From now on you're my family doctor."

"No, no," I said. "I was glad to take care of you because Paul, your lawyer, asked me to. But I am too busy. I am not taking on any new patients."

"You are my family doctor," he said firmly.

"No, I'm not," I said, "but I wish you well. You have a very good physician. Stick with him."

I left the hospital and went back to the office. I told Juanita my bookkeeper; "Mr. Foxfire has been discharged from the hospital so you can bill him. Triple the charge."

There was no insurance at the time.

"What?"

"Triple the charge."

"Doctor," she said, "You can't do that. He's never going to pay."

"That's right," I said, "I hope he doesn't. Triple the charge."

She sent out the bill, and four days later his daughter came in.

"My dad has raved about Dr. Rein," she said, "and I'm here to pay the bill."

She counted out the money in hundred dollar bills on the front desk. My bookkeeper took the money and handed her a receipt.

"I'd like to make an appointment for my son," she said.

"We don't have any appointments for two months," Juanita said. "Can you call back then?"

"Yes, I will," she said.

She never called I'm glad to say. In years to come, Mr. Foxfire, who was known to have associates mysteriously disappear, died of old age in a Federal prison.

Child patients

Early in my practice I had a nice lady come in with her son. When I examined the boy, I could see he was dirty. His underwear was dirty and he had dark dirt around his ankles. It was clear he hadn't bathed in a week.

I looked at her and said, "You know, I really would like to do a thorough examination on him to make sure there's nothing serious going on with him, but he's really dirty. Why don't you go home, give him a bath, change his clothes, and come back so I can do a good examination without being preoccupied with how dirty he is."

You should have seen the look that she gave me.

"She's never coming back," I thought to myself.

Three hours later she and her son were back. The boy was clean. He had clean underwear on. It reminded me of my mother, who once told me, "Before you go to the doctor, always make sure you're wearing clean underwear."

And from then on whenever the boy came to see me, he was clean.

Another time a mother brought in a four-year-old boy with a high fever. He had a bad flu.

"Take him home and give him a cool bath," I said.

That's what the treatment for the flu was at the time. If you put the child in a cool bath for twenty minutes and then threw some ice cubes into the bathtub to make it even cooler, the patient would shake and shake, but the fever would go down until it broke.

She said okay and left. She lived on a street that was on the way to my home, and so that evening I stopped by her house and knocked on the door.

"Hello," she said, "what are you doing here, doctor?"

"I just dropped by to see if you gave your child a cool bath," I said.

"No," she said, "I couldn't do it."

"I can," I said. "May I come in?"

I gave the boy a cool bath for a half an hour.

Before long the entire neighborhood knew the new doctor had made a house call and given the boy a cool bath. I got twenty new patients after I did that.

But that wasn't why I did it. If you do the right thing, there are always dividends. Some they are immediate, and others come over time.

Human connection

Everyone needs angels and gurus. It's just that most people are so pre-occupied with their own thoughts that they don't watch and listen for them. Ordinarily, people look at you but don't see you. Most people are not instinctively insightful. I learned two things over the years that helped me immensely in my medical practice: You can only help some-one if they trust you and accept the advice. To accomplish that, you have to be a good listener.

Sometimes my housekeeper's daughter would come to our house because there was no one to leave her with. I had some toys lying around my office, little puzzles that my grandson and I used to take apart. I showed her how to use them. When she came back she asked me if she could play with the puzzles again.

"Sure, go ahead," I said.

She completed one of the puzzles and was all smiles. She came up to me and said, "I need to tell you something."

"Yes, what is it?"

"My mother says that I am becoming more trustworthy with my toys," she said.

"That's very nice," I said.

"If I keep this up," she said, "she's going to let me go to the mall myself."

A connection is made if you can communicate with a child or a stranger, and if they are willing to tell you something important. Most people don't make such connections unless they are beauticians or manicurists. Why will women tell beauticians all their troubles but they won't discuss them with their husbands at home?

I tried to make connections in my medical practice. Sometimes when a patient came in, she would seem troubled, perhaps by a per-sonal problem. Every once in a while, a patient would cry. And when that happened, I would listen. That's all you have to do, because a good listener is all most people want.

One of the things I teach medical students is to stay until the situation calms down and the person then says, "I'm okay now. Thanks for helping."

Professionals often perform an initial service, whatever that may be, and then say, "Have a nice day. Good bye." And the person who needs the help feels like, *the thing I really came for, the thing I really wanted to talk about, I didn't get to talk about. The professional wasn't interested enough to notice that there was something else on my mind.*

In the case of a doctor, perhaps this was because he or she had a limited amount of time to see the patient. Maybe it was because the particular service was accomplished and the professional then walked out, not giving the patient a chance to talk about what was really on his or her mind.

Every doctor I know says, "Yes, this has happened to me." But how do you give a patient the chance to say what he really wants to say? How do you teach someone to recognize the other person's feelings?

Being a good listener doesn't just happen. It's something you have to train yourself to do. It's a lesson I teach at medical school, "Make sure you listen to your patient carefully and let him finish his sentence…"

Another lesson I learned early: you get more with honey. Once I was flying home to Orlando on Delta Airlines from the Atlanta airport, which is the absolute worst place to be at 11p.m on a day when all the planes are cancelled due to bad weather. All the remaining planes scheduled to fly home were way overbooked. I wasn't even on the standby list.

I walked up to the counter, where people were arguing, shouting, making facial expressions, and had hands balled into fists talking to a harried agent. The agent announced, "Please go to the Delta ticket counter. Vouchers are available for hotel room's overnight and for a meal. We will arrange for you to fly out tomorrow." But that didn't stop the passengers from shouting and pounding their fists.

I stood back, watching and smiling. Finally, after about twenty minutes the passengers in front of me left. I walked up to the agent and smiled.

"I know what you want," she said.

"You have no idea what I want," I replied.

"You want to get home on this flight, don't you?"

"Well, no," I said, "I'm really here because if I don't get home tonight, my wife is going to give me reasons why I need a marriage counselor."

She smiled and said, "Just a minute, step aside for a few minutes."

I stepped aside.

The agent took care of two more people and then handed me a boarding pass for the flight.

"Thank you very much," I said.

"You repay kindness with kindness," she said.

She had been hassled and harassed by everyone else, and I was patient, smiling and knowing she had authority. I made no demands, because by making demands, I wasn't going to get anywhere. She just wanted people to treat her decently. That's all. All it takes is a little kindness.

What a lesson!

I learned how to relate to my patients from a book written by a long-time hero, Lou Holtz, the Notre Dame football coach. I used all his ideas. In short this is how I interpreted his lessons: whenever a patient comes in to see me, or when a lawyer walks into a hearing, or a judge walks in, they need or want something – or at least they think they do. When they look at someone with authority, those in need who are at a disadvantage say to themselves:

Can I trust you?

Will you be honest with me?

If you don't know the answer, will you investigate until you get the right answer instead of just making one up?

After having been schooled by Lou Holtz, whenever a patient came to see me, I knew that patient was asking these three things, and it was my job to assure him or her that yes, I can be trusted. I will be honest. And I won't guess on a diagnosis. Such behavior makes permanent friends. It won't matter if things don't go perfectly, because the patient knows you are on their side and that you won't leave when he or she is in trouble.

The patient also reads your body language. When I teach in medical school, I tell my students, "Do not turn your back on a patient to type into your computer while your patient is talking to you. While your patients are talking to you, look at their eyes and their face."

There is nothing more important at that moment than what your patient is saying. If the patient says, "I have chest pain," or "It hurts in my head," or "My toes tingle when I walk," if you turn around and type on the computer, it's all over. You've lost the patient's trust. Think about people who don't look at you when you're talking to them. They're pre-occupied. They are being talked at, not engaged.

How often have you looked at a waitress while you're talking to her and she's looking back at you, and you think, "She cares more about me than just bringing me hot coffee." It makes you feel that you're a friend.

It's the same in every profession.

When I take on a new employee, I say, "Now that you have a job with me, before you come to work every day I want you to stand in front of the mirror at home and make the ugliest face you can. Pull your cheeks out with your fingers, put your finger in your nose and make ugly faces, and when you think you look silly enough, I want you to laugh. When you're laughing, come to work. I have a terrible time making friends and an easy time making enemies. Your job is to help me make friends." I want them to understand that the most important thing they can cultivate is friendship.

I ask, "Can you smile with your eyes? My father taught me how to do it, and my mother did it naturally. It's a subtle eyebrow lift, a peculiar squint, and a corner of the mouth combination. You either have it, or not. If not, learn it, and once you use it people will communicate with you better and easier. When you get in an elevator, notice the people. Some you will like right away. And some you won't like. You have no idea why. It's instinctual. In the same way a dog can sense whether you like it or not. People are that way too. If a patient doesn't seem to like you when that person walks in the door, don't let that put you off and get in the way of your relationship.

"Practice smiling with your eyes."

CHAPTER 11

MEDICARE

After Medicare came along in July 1965, there was an insurance boom. In the early 1960s, only ten percent of my patients had insurance. By the early 1970s, perhaps seventy-five percent of my patients came to me with insurance. The *New York Times* editorializing about *Medicare and Medicaid at 50*, in 2015, noted,

> At the time the two programs were enacted in July 1965, advocates of Medicare, which today covers 46 million Americans over the age of 65 and nine million younger disabled people, expected that it would expand to cover all Americans. Although polls between 1999 and 2009 showed consistent majorities in favor of expanding Medicare to people between the ages of 55 and 64 to cover more of the uninsured, it never happened... Before Medicare, almost half of all Americans 65 and older had no health insurance. Today that number is two percent. Analysts say that between 1970 and 2010, Medicare contributed to a five-year increase in life expectancy at age 65... those on Medicare are less likely to miss needed care or have unmanageable medical bills... Roughly half of all Medicare recipients live on incomes of less than $24,000 per person... Medicare could be improved by raising its payments to doctors, who often

refuse to take Medicaid patients because the rates are so low compared to private insurance and Medicare.[ii]

Medicare created good and bad, but what I call insurance maneuvering-physicians playing games to maximize cash flow became incredible. Before Medicare and the right for self-employed persons to have retirement plans, I frequently sat in the doctors' lounge outside the operating room and the talk was always, "Is there better suture material than what I am using?" "What clamp are you using?" "This medication is better than what I was using because the patient wakes up quicker."

After the advent of Medicare and private retirement plans, combined with doctors forming 401Ks, most of the talk by doctors turned from helping patients to business plans. Doctors began saying things like, "You know, you can buy an apartment and have all the taxes deductible." Or, "If I put my car into my corporation, then I can have my wife's car expensed out." "My stock broker tells me I shouldn't worry about short-term gains any more. What do you think?"

Those were now the topics of discussion. New ways to manage money and how to save it became a preoccupation. Investment brokers began knocking on our doors, saying things like, "Now that the law has changed, do I have a pension plan for you!" They were as frequent visitors as the ubiquitous drug salesmen who were always coming in trying to sell us different antibiotics, steroids, and other medications.

All this took time away from doctors thinking about their patients. I think it was at this point that medicine became more a business than a profession. Taking care of the *business of medicine* became the first order of business. The professional corporation changed the practice of medicine.

---

ii "Medicare and Medicaid at 50." New York Times, July 3, 2015, Editorial sec.

Surgical groups began because they had more power to negotiate with insurance companies than individual doctors. Blue Cross and Blue Shield grew as competitors to the other insurance companies.

When I started my practice in 1960, about ten percent of my patients had insurance. The cost of my office visit was five dollars. By 1969, over half my patients had insurance and as a sole practitioner I had to take the time to negotiate with the insurance company for my reimbursement. It was exhausting and time consuming.

Medicare ended fifteen years of personalized practice because it stood between my patients and the doctor, and started setting fees. They paid doctors based on what their titles were, what board certification they had, rather than what they did for their patients. That's the way it is now. At that time, a board certified obstetrician was paid $800, for delivery care; but if you were a family doctor you'd only get $350. If you were an ears, nose, and throat guru and did a tonsillectomy, you received $125, and if you were a family doctor you got around $65; and that was insulting to me.

Money was now more important than the professionalism of being a medical doctor. The business side increased in interest, intensity, and pre-occupation, and correspondingly, medical malpractice began to grow as well, much of it occurring because doctors' minds were diverted from the pure practice of medicine. And with litigation came anger and resentment on the part of doctors.

As more doctors turned their attention to money-making, malpractice suits grew. Insurance companies that handled injuries were at a disadvantage. Using my Army experience of evaluating disabilities, I began teaching insurance companies how to recognize bogus claims. Local lawyers who were representing plaintiffs, injured in car accidents or by improper medical care, began asking me to consult. I found that helping attorneys represent patients who were injured was satisfying and lucrative. I also lectured nationally on these subjects, because as a rule, very few doctors will publicly criticize the profession. Soon I developed a large practice assisting patients and lawyers in litigation for injuries.

One day a lawyer who I'd worked with perhaps twenty times called me. The wife of a highly regarded Orange County sheriff officer had hired him.

"Listen, Harry," he said, "a sergeant deputy sheriff just died in Florida Hospital where you work. His wife came to me and said that there was something strange going on. Would you look into it?"

I was about to get a bitter lesson in how the bad guys circle their wagons. It was a lesson that would have great impact on my future.

The deputy sheriff had a motorcycle accident and needed a leg amputated but died on the operating table. He was a big healthy, strong guy, and his wife didn't like the explanation for his death. My lawyer friend asked, "Can you check out the cause of death and let me know, so I can tell her?"

Given the balance between protecting the doctor who might have screwed up and my sense of fairness to the deputy sheriff, I overcame my reluctance and political good sense, and agreed to help.

I went to the hospital medical records department. Everyone knew me; I had been a busy member of the staff fourteen years. It was a small hospital.

"Can I see the records of Sergeant So-and-so?" I asked.

They said sure and gave me his records. Three pages piqued my interest. "Would you make me copies of these three pages?" I asked.

They did.

The next day I went back to the lawyer's office and said, "I think these are important pages. You should get an anesthesiologist to look at them, because there are a few things here that don't look right. I'm not an expert in the field, but what I'm seeing tells me something's wrong. You should get it checked out."

He did. The records showed that an anesthesiologist had combined the wrong medications, which resulted in the patient dying instantly. It was a known drug contraindication. My lawyer friend told the widow and she filed a lawsuit for malpractice. Three months later he took the deposition of the anesthesiologist who had since produced a different document. At the end of the deposition the doctor was shown his original sheet, which he had completely rewritten. Doctors do this all the time and often get away with the medical wrongdoing. But since I had a copy of the original, his duplicity was there for all to see.

"Is this your signature?" the doctor was asked when shown the sheet I had copied.

"Yes."

"Is this the anesthesia sheet?"

"Yes."

The lawyer then produced the original.

The defendant doctor, caught red-handed, caved. The case was settled the next day for what was then a substantial sum.

Five days later I got a certified letter on my desk that said, "You are hereby suspended from Florida Hospital. If you wish to appeal, you can appear Tuesday afternoon at five o'clock at a special board meeting for this purpose."

I went.

"Do you have an idea why you're here?" I was asked. I had an idea.

"Did you look at the records in this case?"

"Yes."

"Did you copy the records?"

"No," I said. "I asked the medical records department to copy them for me."

"And did you give those to a lawyer?"

"Yes."

"Why?"

"The sergeant's widow hired a lawyer who hired me to evaluate them."

"Did you have permission to look at the records?"

"I did."

"Did you bring written permission?"

"No, I didn't bring written permission. I had permission. Everyone knows me here."

"And that's why you did it, because you took advantage of us and you caused this doctor a great deal of grief?"

"I don't think I caused him as much grief as much as he caused the wife by killing the sergeant with the wrong medication," I said.

"Well, you're hereby suspended."

When I returned the other doctors made it very clear that they didn't want me around them. It was so obvious that one day when I almost cut off my thumb with a power saw in my garage, I chose to operate on it myself in my office instead of going to the hospital.

One Sunday I was working in my garage with a power saw and I wasn't paying attention. The saw blade went halfway through my thumb below the knuckle. The tip was hanging off. I rushed into the house with blood gushing.

The first thing you have to do is thoroughly clean it; because if you don't, exposed bone could risk osteomyelitis, and if you get that, it's six months of trouble. I stood at the sink for about a half hour. My thumb was as clean as a baby's tush.

When Rhea and my daughter Debra came home, they saw blood all over the floor. Rhea asked, "What happened?"

"I'm rinsing off my thumb," I said.

"We are going to the emergency room to get it fixed," Rhea said.

"No, we're not," I said.

"Please, let's go to the emergency room," she pleaded.

"We are not going to the emergency room," I repeated.

"What are you going to do?" she asked.

"I'm going to fix it myself," I said. "Debra's a nurse. You're my assistant. We're going to the office."

Rhea got out all the instruments and Debra handed me the ones I needed. I gave myself a shot to numb the pain and after that it was just a matter of putting the stitches in right. With one hand, I sewed up my thumb and Debra tied the stitches, today you can't even see a mark.

I worked at the hospital on and off for the next two years. On one occasion, Rhea was admitted into the hospital. We were going to wait to see whether or not she needed surgery. Twenty-four hours after admission her surgeon said, "I can't wait anymore. We better do it."

He called down to the operating room, and said, "We're going to do surgery on Rhea Rein." The word came back, "You are not going to do surgery on Rhea Rein in this hospital because none of the ten anesthesiologists in this hospital is available to do her surgery."

"Why?" the operating staff member was asked.

"Because she's Dr. Rein's wife."

With tubes coming out of every orifice in her body and intravenous medication in each arm, we had no choice but to transfer her to Winter Park Hospital, where she had surgery and recovered. This event became headlines on the front pages of many newspapers around the country.

I sued and ten anesthesiologists got together in one deposition. They circled the wagons. They swore that at the time my wife needed surgery they all were busy with emergency procedures.

They lied and they beat me. Something had to change, and the easiest thing to change was my modus operandi, because unfortunately sometimes you can't change the world. The angel that helped Rhea recover now turned to steer me back on course.

CHAPTER 12

HOSPITAL WARS

As the 1970s progressed, I spent much of my time fighting hospital bureaucracy. I found out the hard way that when you work in a hospital, you have to be a talented politician.

When I moved to Orlando I joined the staffs of four different hospitals. For each hospital you had to apply for staff privileges, and after two or three weeks, you would get them. Hospitals need doctors, and if you're a doctor who is bringing patients into the hospital, that's profit for the hospital. So it was routine. But I encountered problems when I requested privileges for performing procedures that only specialists are supposed to do and which general practitioners like me were ordered not to do.

Whenever a hospital board refused to allow me to operate, I would fight them. I went to war on a regular basis against hospital administrators to prove I had the skills, talent and experience to operate, based on my documented army training. About twice a year it would result in me being called before the hospital executive committee to justify a procedure I was doing that a specialist didn't want me to do. He wanted me to refer my patient to him. I wasn't doing anything dramatic. I was delivering babies. Fortunately, the chief of obstetrics at Florida Hospital had enough work and was supportive. The problem came when he stepped down and his successor didn't like me doing obstetrics.

Another brouhaha came after I began performing tonsillectomies on children. I had done dozens of them in the army. Taking kids' tonsils out was very popular in the late 1960s. The ears, nose, and throat specialists didn't like it, but they had plenty of work, and so they mildly told me, "You shouldn't do them," but I did them anyway.

At the end of a tonsillectomy procedure, you have to ensure there is no bleeding from the adenoids. If there is, you have to bring the child back to the operating room, and it's a headache for the hospital, the operating room staff, the parents, and the doctor. You have to put the child under anesthesia again, which is more dangerous than doing it the first time. I had developed a technique to ensure there was no blood in the back of the throat behind the soft palate and the nose. This technique used a suction tube in the nose and liquid in the mouth to see if the color changed as you sent liquid up the soft palate and out the nose. If the color gets light and watery instead of staying pink, then you know there's no blood oozing. In the Army my technique became known as the "Rein Sign." I taught it to nurses at the private hospitals where I worked.

One day I got a call to appear before the executive committee of the Florida Hospital.

"Are you doing tonsillectomies, sir?"

"Yes, sir."

"Are you trained to do that, sir?"

"Yes, sir."

"Dr. L. is an ear, nose, and throat doctor, and he lodged a complaint. After he did a tonsillectomy on one of his patients, one of the nurses asked, 'Did you check the Rein Sign?' He was told, 'Look to see if there's bleeding in the adenoids. Dr. Rein does that all the time.'"

It turned out that the reason I was before the executive committee was because they were angry that I had named a procedure after myself. "Why would you name a technique after yourself?" I was asked.

"Because I don't think anyone in this hospital would name it after me," I said.

"Well, you're not supposed to do that."

"I never realized that you can't name anything after yourself," I said. Tempers rose.

"No one has to call it the Rein Sign," I said. "They don't have to call it anything. I didn't publish it any place. I am doing surgery. The nurses and I are friends. If you don't want me to call it the Rein Sign any more, so be it. Don't you good people have more to do than to make me waste my entire morning out of my office for this purpose?"

I wasn't polite and it led to more hostility.

Choose the hill you want to die on

Not long after this, one of my patients came to see me, "I've been your patient for a long time," he said, "and you look distressed. I read the article in the paper about their refusal to operate on your wife. Is this why you look down?"

"Yes," I admitted.

"What are you going to do about it?" he asked.

"I don't know."

"Do you have time for a story," he asked.

I did.

"I was a master sergeant in the Korean War," he began, "and on a regular basis second lieutenants would come out of West Point to our division. I was assigned to them. The quickest way for a second lieutenant to become a first lieutenant is if he takes an important hill. And that makes more room for other second lieutenants.

"A company is made up of platoons, and my platoon had many men killed and injured following counter-productive orders over a few months. At a certain point I decided I wasn't about to do this anymore. We were taking hills that weren't very important just so some officers could get promoted. So from then on when we were ordered to take a hill, I would order my platoon to stand down, and I would explain to the men in the platoon why the hill had no strategic value. After the discussion I would say to my men, 'Is this the hill for which you are willing to die?'

"And you know, Doc, when you get into trouble for things like this, you have to decide, is this the hill you want to die on? It's an old military saying but it is an important one: is this the battle you want to fight? If it is, you better fight it to win and if not, use your energy in a different way."

After that, anytime I experienced a crisis with the hospital, I would ask myself, "Is this the hill you want to die on?"

Diphtheria

One time I had a patient who was very sick. None of the medication I prescribed worked. I arrived at the hospital in the middle of the afternoon to see him and he was complaining bitterly. I checked his throat and saw something I had seen only once before – diphtheria.

I took a culture and sent it to the lab. I left instructions to check for diphtheria, which closes the upper portion of the trachea. My patient began to choke and I could see he needed a tracheotomy, which means you have to put a tube in the trachea just below the thyroid so he can breathe. I called for help from two specialists.

"Why?" they asked.

"Because he has diphtheria and if we don't do this now, he can choke to death," I said.

"Harry," one of the doctors said, "he doesn't have diphtheria. We don't see it any longer. You're in a dream world."

"Have a nice day," said the other one.

He wasn't *their* patient. It was late in the afternoon, and they didn't want to be bothered. My problem was that even though I had done tracheotomies in medical school, I didn't have the authority to do one in the hospital. This time I didn't care. I knew if I didn't do it, my patient would die.

"Get a tracheotomy set," I ordered the nurses. Even though most tracheotomies are done in an operating room, you can do it while a patient is in his ward bed.

I performed the operation and immediately the patient began breathing easier.

He smiled at me. He couldn't talk, but I could see he was grateful.

I told him, "You'll be here for at least two weeks and you'll have intravenous antibiotics for most of that time."

He nodded that he understood. Forty years later I was with my grandson at an Orlando Magic basketball game and a man came running up to us. I recognized him immediately.

"Your grandfather saved my life," he told my grandson. "I had diphtheria and no one believed him."

Not long after I performed that tracheotomy, I had another patient, a man very well known around town, who attempted suicide. He swallowed an entire bottle of Seconal and wound up in a different hospital across town. I got a call to see him and when I arrived he looked terrible. I gave him supportive treatment until the Seconal wore off - it usually takes about eighteen hours. My problem was that I didn't know when he swallowed the pills, so it was still possible the effects hadn't yet peaked. He could get better or worse, only time would tell.

I pondered whether or not to go home, but I decided that he was not going to die on my watch, and I stayed with him the entire night. Around three in the morning I took his pulse and I could see it was slowing. His respirations were down to almost nothing.

He needed an urgent tracheotomy. I called the support staff and told them what I needed and as in the other hospital I was told no.

"If he's lived this long," I was told by the doctor I consulted, "he'll be okay. We'll see him in the morning." It was because Dr. Rein was calling that they didn't want to come. So my patient would pay the price for an attitude toward me unless I acted. Once again I performed a tracheotomy. In the morning, after the Seconal had finally worn off, he recovered. Three days later when I removed the tracheostomy, Bill thanked me profusely and swore he would never again attempt to take his life.

In separate meetings executive committees at both hospitals had me appear before them for performing a tracheotomy, which I did not have privileges to perform. After I explained each situation my question was, "What would you say to me if I hadn't done it and the patient died?"

"He wouldn't have died," each told me.

"That's the whole point," I said. "We don't know whether he would have lived without the procedure."

"That's not what you're here for," I was lectured. "You're here because we're charging you with doing a surgical procedure in our hospital for which you had no privilege." They felt I was giving them the middle finger, and so I was officially warned. Once again I ate humble pie. You have to know when to hold and when to fold. If you eat humble pie, you live to fight another day.

After too many fights with hospital bureaucrats, I almost entirely stopped doing hospital work. The word was out: "You know, Rein is helping plaintiff's lawyers in malpractice cases and he's looking at records he doesn't have the right to look at."

It wasn't true, but that was the word. For a year and a half, I didn't do any hospital work.

Around this time, I learned that one of my best friends, Alex Maybarduk, a surgeon, was deathly ill at Florida Hospital. He was a patient in my family practice, but he was in the hospital because of abnormal lung x-ray findings. Alex owned a large house on extensive property on a lake in Orlando and every time a stray dog or cat wandered over, he'd take it in. At one time they sent me their Vietnamese housekeeper who became very ill. I took an x-ray and she had what looked like pneumonia. She had no money and no insurance.

I told her, "I want you to come into my office every morning at 9 o'clock. Each morning for a week I'm going to hang a bottle of intravenous fluid with medication in it and feed it into your arm."

She showed up each morning and I fed her antibiotics intravenously for a week, and by the end of that time she was cured. Alex was ever grateful. This occurred several years before Alex became very ill.

It was difficult for me to go to the hospital when his wife called because I was still locked in conflict with the hospital administrators, but still, he was my friend, I went to the hospital and into his room. I closed the door. His wife told me that he had just had some x-rays taken. The radiologist said cancer had spread to his lungs and that she should make sure his will was in order, because he was going to go quickly.

"Who's the radiologist?" I asked.

She told me. To my mind the man was not skilled and had made many inaccurate diagnoses. "First of all," I said, "I wouldn't believe anything that man says."

"Look at Alex's records," she said.

"I can't," I said. "If the nurses see me, they'll call the administrators, and we'll start this war all over again. Why don't you let Alex look at his own records and I'll look at them with him?"

She went outside and told the nurses, "My husband would like to see his records."

They gave her the records and she brought them into the room. I looked at them. "Something's not right here," I said. "Why don't we take Alex up to the University of Florida and I'll have one of my friends or one of his friends look at this and tell him what to do?"

"I shouldn't leave here against the advice of my doctor," Alex said, "He's very, very proper. He's a good friend and my surgeon, and my wife's surgeon. He'll be angry."

"If you die," I said, "it really doesn't matter what your proper doctor thinks about you. And if you don't die, then it still doesn't matter what your doctor thinks because he was wrong."

"Well," Alex said, "they can't get me into the University of Florida."

"Let me make a few phone calls," I said.

There was a waiting list, but not when I explained.

"When can you get him here?" I was asked.

"In about three hours," I said.

"How are you going to get me there in three hours?" asked Alex.

"We are going to take the blankets from your bed and your wife is going to carry two pillows. We'll put them in my station wagon and I'm going to drive you there."

"How are you going to get me to the station wagon?"

"There's something called a wheelchair," I said.

And that's exactly what we did. I wheeled him to my car, and we drove to Gainesville. After three hours of driving, we arrived at about 6:30pm. The doctor there looked at the x-rays and declared, "I haven't got the slightest idea what this shows." He did a biopsy of Alex' lung and around ten pathologists looked at it, half said it was cancer and the other half said it wasn't. By chance there was a pathologists' convention in Las Vegas and so they took the slides to Las Vegas. Again, half the pathologists thought it was cancer and half didn't.

I said to them, "Let me tell you about Alex's housekeeper from Vietnam."

After I told them the story they said, "It's nothing like that."

"Maybe not," I said, "but why don't you give this man some antibiotics in an IV for a week and see what happens."

"He doesn't need it."

"Well, why don't you give them to him anyway?" I said.

"Because it has all sorts of side effects."

"We'll there's no side effects if you die and if you think he's dying anyway, why don't you give him the antibiotic for the hell of it?"

"Harry, you're so full of it," Alex said. "You know you're always full of ideas, and none of them ever work."

"They worked on your housekeeper and your dog," I said.

He had also had a dog that was sick, and I managed to cure him as well, and that's the argument that got him. So they put Alex on powerful antibiotics and within a week his lung cleared. Four months later Alex was better and he went back to work. Twelve years later Alex died of diabetes. There is a further post-script to this story, Alex' son Gary, became the Undersecretary of State of Economic Affairs in South America. Many years after Alex died, I was at a wedding and ran into Gary. He again thanked me for saving his father's life. During our conversation I talked about how much I loved my Army career. Five months later I received an invitation from the Army War College, which teaches strategic thinking of complex military issues. They also have intensive programs for civilians who can clear Top Secret ranking and who are high achievers. I went to the last ten days of one of those courses. Although lectures were attended by sixty students, each student has daily discussions tutors. One of the instructors was the lead tank commander in both Iraq wars. I asked, "I keep up with politics, but why did we *really* go into Iraq?"

"That question has been asked over and over again by different people," he said, "but it hasn't been asked by anyone in this class yet."

He pulled down a huge map of the Middle East. In brief he said that the Prophet Mohammed predicted that there would be twelve caliphs, or spiritual leaders, all of them from the Quays tribe after his death. He said too that imposters would also proclaim themselves as caliphs. The only two caliphs recognized in both Sunni and mainstream Shi'a Islam are Ali ibn Abu Talib (656 – 661) and Hasan ibn Ali (661). However, the U.S. military wanted to prevent a new caliphate from forming. We failed to prevent it because a new caliphate, as manifested by the Islamic State, has announced itself, it is an ultra-conservative group of Muslims who seek total control of the Middle East and of the world. It is a group widely rejected by mainstream Islam.

Because I was invited to the War College, I was able to understand their outlook on the war, which was full of insights and predictions of that now happening daily. Just being there for those ten days was a thrill and a highlight of my life.

Getting away

Persistent challenges at work and with some of my other business interests, including holdings in a construction and mortgage company were wearing me down. My friend, Howard, who was moving from a well-paying job in the pharmaceutical industry to the financial industry was also tense.

We decided to do something to ease the strain. I had bought a 21-foot cabin cruiser, and we decided to go on an adventure. We would cruise from the waters in Palm Beach all the way down through the Florida Keys to Key West. We had passed the Power Squadron course and courses from the Coast Guard in navigation and saw ourselves as invincible seamen. Veritable Vikings. We had no radio, no radar, and cell phones didn't yet exist. We had life preservers but no flares. We weren't as smart as we thought we were.

The first night we dropped anchor under a bridge in Boca Raton. We lay on the beds in the bow of the boat, only to be attacked by a million mosquitos. We sprayed the cabin with a cloud of mosquito repellent. The mosquitoes died and we almost did too as clouds of choking spray entered our lungs. When I woke up the next morning I felt a sharp pain in my back. I asked Howard to look at it. He said it looked like an insect bite. Lying on the bunk was a dead spider. I wondered whether it was an omen.

Once out of Miami, we were on our own without communication of any kind and often with no land in sight. Using a navigation map, the compass, and following the channel markers, we reached the island of Marathon. As I got close to the dock, I cut the engine, and we glided in to refuel. It was shallow, so I lifted the engine out of the water.

A woman standing on the shore asked when I had bought my new jet engine. I asked her what she was talking about.

"Your engine has no propeller," she said, "I assumed it was a jet engine."

To my horror I could see that our propeller was missing. We had scuba gear on board and dived looking for the propeller. Howard swam out of sight. He was about fifty yards away, around the corner of the dock.

"Why are you looking over there, Howard?" I asked. "You're nowhere near the boat."

"There's more light here," he said.

That phrase became a catchword between Howard, me, and our friends for many years. Whenever someone would say something silly or inappropriate, the answer back would always be, "There's more light here."

I'm happy to say we found the propeller lying in the silt not far from the boat. A shear pin had broken and we needed a new one. It was a Sunday and all the boat repair shops on Marathon Key were closed. We rented a hotel room, stayed overnight, and bought a replacement part the next morning and set off again. We were cruising comfortably to Key West, out in the open water about three miles off-shore, when suddenly the boat jarred to a stop. I cut the engine. We had run aground on a sand bar.

Howard and I jumped off the side of the boat and tried to pull it and push it off. The sand bar was very narrow. If I stepped back only a couple of feet on either side of the boat, the water was over our head. Nor were we sure if the tide was going out or coming in.

We waited and were lucky. Within an hour we floated free. I started the engine, and we made it to Key West without further incident. We were tired, thirsty, and sunburned, and we had second thoughts about the return trip. We discussed selling the boat in Key West, eating the loss, and taking a bus back home. Or even just abandoning the boat and taking the bus back home.

First we had to decide what to do with the boat. We saw a Holiday Inn down the beach. Near it was a pole in the water about twelve feet high. The water was only about three feet deep and so we tied the boat to the pole. We waded ashore with our suitcases over our heads and headed for the comfort of newly made beds with fresh linens.

Howard and I looked like pirates in bathing suits when we walked into the lobby of the hotel. We hadn't shaved and I'm sure we smelled pretty bad. When the clerk at the desk looked at us, I could see by his expression that we did not look like desirable guests. We told him what had happened and after I showed him my credentials, he reluctantly gave us a room. I can't describe how wonderful it was to take a hot shower, feel clean sheets, and sleep in a bed free of spiders and swarms of mosquitoes.

By now Howard and I had completely forgotten our troubles at home, which seemed trivial compared to the challenges of our trip. We talked and laughed about it and made it back home without further incident. Was there an angel on that boat? Considering our boating skills, there had to be.

CHAPTER 13

MOVING ON

Askiing accident in 1974 helped determine the new course my life would take. I love to ski and usually went to Colorado. In that year I went with a cousin and three very good friends. Before we headed up the mountain in a gondola, I, as the most experienced member of the group said, "You wait down here. I want to check the slopes to see which we'll ski on."

I had just bought a new pair of expensive skis and boots. I installed the bindings myself. That was a big mistake. I adjusted the bindings so the boots were certain not to easily come out of the bindings. I started down the mountain. Veering off slope, I slid into deep powder. The tip of one of my skis dipped down into the powder and I flipped forward. I had twelve fractures of my tibia. Someone called the ski patrol and I was taken to the hospital. They took x-rays which they hung in front of me. They say that doctors and nurses make the worst patients and I was about to become an example of that.

"Oh my God," I said to the doc, "That's not me, is it?"

"Yes," he said, "and you know what we're going to have to do? You're going to need surgery to nail and pin the fractures. First we will cut off the boot."

"Don't cut off the boot," I said. "I just bought them," and then I said, "No surgery."

"We're going to operate," he said.

"No, you're not."

"We do a lot of surgeries around here."

"Just set it properly," I said. "No surgery."

He set it. I lay in bed. My cousin and two friends had no idea where I was. They figured I had gone off and skied on my own and that they'd catch up with me for dinner.

It was now five in the afternoon, and I was coming out of anesthesia. I picked up the phone and called the hotel clerk to put a note on their door that said something like, "I've broken my neck, but you guys don't give a damn. Hope you're having a good time."

They showed up with flowers. What was I going to do with flowers?

The doctor set the leg and put me in a cast. I was in agony, but I didn't know why. Whenever I'd howl in pain, I'd get another shot of morphine. The surgeon said I would get better soon, but for seven days I was on an intravenous morphine drip as I screamed in pain.

It turned out the reason I was in such pain was that he had put the cast on too tight. And by the time I was discharged I was a morphine addict. I got over that in a week because I knew what was happening. But it took about four months for me to figure out that my main problem was a result of the cast being put on too tight. It was squeezing the sciatic nerve in the back of my thigh.

After the accident I worked part time for a year and a half. I was sure I'd never walk properly again. I was in agony the whole time. I gave myself the diagnosis of Causalgia, which is a severe burning pain brought on by injury to a nerve outside the spinal cord. I hated that diagnosis. The only time I got relief, strangely enough, was when I smoked, or watched the *Tonight Show* or *Star Trek*, or professional wrestling on television, particularly wrestler Dusty Rhodes with his bionic elbow.

We put a hospital bed in my room at home so I could elevate different parts of my body. I was sure I'd never work again, though after three or four months I could hop around. I then began working part-time.

I hired doctors from the local naval base as my substitutes to keep my practice functional. I told them, "Your job is to keep my patients happy and to do a good job in medicine. Whatever comes in is yours, I'm not taking a cut of it. I need you to keep my practice alive."

And they did. My nurses were instructed, "Any time a patient needs to talk to me or wants to ask me a question, give them my number and have them call me." I received calls six or seven times a day. My patients stayed very loyal, they knew I cared about them.

It was the malpractice of the doctor who had put on my cast too tight and who gave me morphine for the pain that got me thinking about the world of medical malpractice. I now understood personal injury from a very personal place.

The severity of my fractures, the less than rapid recovery, and attitudes I recognized in multiple specialists as a patient, in addition to not being able to do hospital work because of my infirmity, resulted in a change of practice from family care to trauma evaluation and management. I studied methods of disability evaluation, grounded in my studies of US Army disability discharge procedures. Two books for lawyers and insurance companies followed, *The Primer on Soft Tisue Injuries* and *Medical Malpractice Thoughtbook*. I went on the lecture circuit and was soon called on as an expert witness testifying in injury cases in medical malpractice trials.

Another venture into publishing was a twelve-hour tape series and from that I was hired to consult to many insurance companies in case evaluation. I told them, "You're always worried about patients trying to cheat you or to take more money from you than they deserve by making too many claims. But there are bad doctors, just like there are bad lawyers and bad chiropractors, but to become paranoid over this gets you nowhere. Instead, you would be better off learning how to evaluate records to discover what's not credible and not believable."

I started to heal and after the cast came off, I limped around. After a while I could drive to the insurance companies and consult with them. I was happy to get the work because it kept my mind active and it wasn't long before I became the national consultant to Prudential Property and Casualty Company, one of the larger insurance companies. I also consulted for State Farm, Nationwide, Continental Casualty, and more.

But as insurance companies trusted my advice more, my relationships with the doctors at the hospitals where I worked became hostile. As time went by, every time I helped a plaintiff's lawyer in a case against a doctor, in any of many states that I traveled, word would come back to the hospitals where I worked. I would be met with anger from the other doctors. I would get frequent inflammatory, bitter phone calls.

Rhea had always been active in Hadassah, an American Jewish Women's organization that raises funds for hospitals among other charitable efforts. One afternoon she went to a fund-raiser and was sitting at a table opposite the mother of a doctor, someone neither of us knew. The woman stood up and said for all to hear, "I'm not sitting at this table. She's Dr. Rein's wife."

Rhea has never gotten over it.

As the doctors ostracized me, I began realizing it was because some feared the truth, they'd been so accustomed to burying their mistakes, and now they were being questioned, as we all should be.

Understanding Malpractice

Medical malpractice was first discussed in the Old Testament. The Torah and the Koran talk about restitution. Did you cause injury to someone else? If you did, you are required to fix it or pay for it. Of course, there are all kinds of injuries. Whether you trampled on someone's flowers or poked someone in the eye, that's an injury according to the Old Testament.

Today we call it personal injury or medical malpractice. We read the headlines in the newspapers. What really seems to bother people are the verdicts and large judgments the victims receive. But the way I see it, what really bothers many people is that someone else is getting the money.

In the late 1970s, I had a patient who was in intensive care. At the time I was teaching nurses how to listen to lungs and to correlate pulse, blood pressure, and what causes elevation or falls. One night I received a call from a nurse I didn't know well about a very sick patient of mine. She described a symptom to me and if this had been twenty years earlier, I would have come running to the hospital, which was only about six minutes away. This time I told her, "Get an x-ray, get some blood work, and call me back."

Patients in intensive care frequently have blood pressure that drops making them difficult to arouse. You have to determine a patient's capacity for sustaining himself while his treatment is being managed.

As I lay in bed barking instructions, my wife asked, "You're not going in?"

"No," I said. "She'll run some tests, and she'll get back to me if there's a problem."

After evaluating the tests over the phone, I told the nurse I'd be in later that morning.

"You're really not going in?" my wife asked me.

"No," I said, "I'll see her in the morning."

The next day I went in to see my patient. My wife, asked me about her. "Everything's fine," I said. "She's doing well, and she didn't need me."

"You know," she said, "you've never done that before."

With that one statement, "You've never done that before," my life changed. Why didn't I go in? Not going in to personally administer my patient meant that I was not as careful as I should have been with that patient. For someone with my personality, it was out of character, and on reflection, totally unacceptable. Years later when I taught young doctors, I added that experience to my definition of malpractice.

Moving On

In 1979, I hired Jan Becker, a super smart and dedicated internist. I told him, "Your job is to take great care of patients and not to worry about the business of medicine. If you can do that, this practice will take care of you."

When he began he was board certified in Internal Medicine. When he would interpret an EKG in the office, often I would read it and explain something he might have missed. He was good, but he lacked experience. Insurance paid him $75 for an EKG reading, while it paid me $35, as a family physician, for the same reading. I was getting more and more frustrated by these tariff differences.

However, I was becoming fulfilled by my lecturing, teaching insurance companies about injury evaluation and medical record interpretation, and with being needed by lawyers who had to fight the medical establishment. By now I was good at that. Moreover, I was paid well for my out of the office advice, and so I decided to leave medicine and go to law school.

The next year I gave Jan the practice without charging him for it. I had been in practice for twenty-three years. Jan has now been in practice for more than three decades and he plans to stay there until he retires.

CHAPTER 14

MEDICINE AND LAW

In 1975, I went to a national convention of the Association of Trial Lawyers of America. I needed to learn. I wanted to see who the leading litigators were, and to be seen by them. The trip was life changing.

At the convention I handed out flyers for my *Primer on Soft Tissue Injuries*. I was hoping I could speak there, because when you lecture, people think you're an expert, and if they think you're an expert, they will hire you. It is extremely difficult to get on one of the programs at the Association of Trial Lawyers of America, but if you just show up you never know what can happen.

I was at a cocktail party at the convention talking to Stanley Chesley, one of prime trial lawyers of the time. It was late into the night when Stanley took a call and returned sullen.

"What happened?" I asked.

"My keynote speaker just called," he said. "He can't come tomorrow." Then he said, "You've just written a book. Would you like to speak instead of him tomorrow at eleven?"

'Yes," I said.

That's how opportunities happen. I went back to my room. I didn't sleep the rest of the night preparing my speech on how to prove damages in a personal injury case. I discussed how to bring believable proof to a jury and how to make sure the jury doesn't think your client is exaggerating.

I gave it all I had and it was a hit. I sold a lot of books, and when I arrived home, my talk made the telephone ring. As a result of that presentation, I gave seminars around the United States and in five other countries over the next twenty years.

My patient and good friend, Marvin Newman, a lawyer in Orlando and a professor at Rollins College, was teaching law enforcement seminars each Saturday morning. One day he called and asked if I would stand in for him.

"I'd love to," I said.

"By the way," he said, "the dean will be sitting in on the class."

I suppose this was to make sure Marvin hadn't picked some joker to teach this important class. I over-prepared for the class. I started at nine in the morning. The room was rectangular and it ran slightly uphill so all the people in the back could see. There was a big clock on the back wall.

I began and at 10 o'clock, sharp, I finished.

There was silence. No one got up to leave.

From the front of the room one of the students said to me, "Dr. Rein, did Mr. Newman tell you this is a three-hour class?"

I had finished my talk two hours early. I had said everything for which I prepared. I had to think quickly.

"Doesn't Mr. Newman ordinarily give you a break during the three hours?" I said to the class. "Why don't we take ten minutes?"

I was breathing deeply. My hands were sweaty. My armpits were dripping. After ten minutes the students returned. I had to talk for another two hours on preparing to be an expert witness, what "expert" really should mean, and how to regain composure if it looks like disaster is about to strike.

Around two in the afternoon I could see the students getting restless and I wrapped it up. The dean came over.

"Harry, you sure can talk," he said.

"I didn't even get to talk about the malpractice cases," I said.

"I'd like to hear that," he said.

"Pick the time," I said.

"Okay, how about Monday morning?"

"I'll talk to you Monday morning."

From little acorns do big oaks grow. Deans and educators talk to each other and over the next few weeks I was invited to speak one Saturday a month about medical jurisprudence at the University of Florida College of Law.

Marvin was good friends with the dean. One day I told Marvin how much I wanted to go to law school and he said, "Well, let me call the dean and talk to him about it."

He introduced us by phone, and I went to see him.

The dean said, "You've been in medical practice for twenty years and you have no idea what law school is all about. You will have to take the LSATs, the law school aptitude test required by state law. If it's already been given this year, you'll have to wait another six months to take it."

"Is there any way I can take the test now to be ready for your first class?"

"I don't know," he said.

"Let me call Princeton," I said.

The Scholastic Aptitude Test offices are based there.

They told me, "We can give the test at the University of Central Florida. You'll have to hire a tutor and you'll have to rent a room. We can FedEx the test to the tutor who has to be with you at all times for the whole day. After you take the test, the tutor will have to FedEx the test back to us."

The University of Central Florida was a half an hour from my home. They charged me forty dollars for the room and the tutor cost me twelve dollars an hour for six hours. I took the exam and the tutor sent it back to Princeton. A day and a half later the results were sent to the dean at the law school. I went to see him.

"I have never seen a grade on the LSATs this low," he said. "What did you do, guess?"

"Yes," I said, "I guessed on most of them."

"This is the lowest score I've ever seen as the dean here," he said, "but the requirement is that you *take* the test. There is no requirement that you get a good grade on it. You're accepted into the law school if you want to be here, Harry."

We shook hands.

When I told my wife Rhea what I intended to do, she was furious. I was scheduled to start law school in January of 1980 and to do that we would have to move a hundred miles north from Orlando to Gainesville. Complicating things, my second daughter Debra was getting married in the spring.

Rhea didn't want to move and she didn't want me commuting over a hundred miles each way either. Moreover, she said, "you have the largest, busiest medical practice in Central Florida and for you to give this all away is just crazy. How can you just leave your practice?"

It led to the worst three weeks of our marriage.

One morning I was shaving, and I was reminded of what had happened back in 1958. I had just been promoted to captain in the Army, making $400 a month with a house with all my utilities paid and living in total comfort. We had one wonderful child and were planning another, and we were as happy as could be, when Martin, an Army doctor friend of mine, said we could double our salaries if we became doctors for Airborne and the Rangers. Why not? All we had to do was jump out of an airplane once a month and we could make an extra $400 a month.

I leapt at the chance. Martin and I went to the officer's club where we bought Ranger and Airborne uniform patches. When you become a Ranger, you become a really big deal in the Army, especially if you're a doctor.

"We're rich," I said to my wife.

"What are you talking about?" she said.

"Could you please sew these patches on my jacket?"

She knew that it meant I would be jumping from airplanes.

"Are you crazy?" she said. "You come home describing the horrible injuries you treat from the guys who jump out of planes. They land in trees and branches go through their trachea, they break their legs, and you want to put yourself through that?"

"You only have to jump once a month," I said.

"We have one child, and you want to have another one? Well, I don't want a crippled husband."

She was so upset I walked across the courtyard to talk to Martin, and who did I see walking toward my apartment? Martin, we were both shaking our heads. His wife had the same reaction. He was a surgeon in the unit and he had been telling his wife similar stories.

And so as I was shaving, I was thinking back to what I had given up, because of Rhea's concern for me. I finished shaving and I said to her, "This has been a pretty miserable three weeks. But let me tell you what I was thinking about while I was shaving." I told her about how she had prevented me from becoming a Ranger.

"Someday," I said, "when I'm 60 or 70 or 80 and shaving, I don't want to say to myself, *I could have gone to law school if it hadn't been for my wife*. I don't ever want you to be in that position."

"Harry, you're right," she said.

On that same day we bought a condominium in Gainesville. I bought a new car, five shirts and two pairs of jeans, the accepted law student clothing of the day. We furnished the condo, and I went to law school. And while I was in law school, Rhea went to paralegal school.

I was the oldest person in the law school, except for one professor who was teaching torts, one of the litigation specialties. I thought it would be nice to befriend him. I was determined to learn more from his experiences.

In most universities there is something I call form over substance, which means you learn a lot of facts but not how to apply them. It was much more important to me at that stage of life to learn the law that applies to medical malpractice and injury and drug litigation, rather than know details about contracts, bonds, taxation, apartment houses and floods.

I befriended the professor who liked the idea that he had an older student to talk to, but on the third day of law school he died. I told the dean how sad I was. The dean said, "Here was a man who was an academic his entire life, saved very little money and all his wife has is her small house, and an insurance policy of $250,000."

"What happened?" I asked.

"He had a heart attack, slipped in his bathroom and hit his head on the commode and died."

"I hope he had double indemnity," I said.

"It wasn't an accident," said the dean.

"Dean, he slipped, hit his head, and had a heart attack."

The autopsy done on him by the pathologist at the University of Florida reported a heart attack resulting in a fall and him hitting his head.

"He's not correct," I said. "Why don't we write the insurance company a letter, and you can say you have the former medical examiner of Orange County, Florida review his file, and that the correct series of events was that he slipped on the wet floor in the bathroom, hit his head, and had a heart attack. Then you can say, "Obviously, this will be easy to prove using all the knowledge and skill of all the lawyers at the University of Florida College of Law."

"Let's do that," he said.

The next day I had a letter ready. He sent it in to the insurance company, and in another thirty days the professor's wife had another check for an additional $250,000.

The dean and I became friends. The lesson I taught was that you don't question people's personality or their motives, but you question what they put down on paper. Never lie, never add facts that don't exist, accurately portray what happened. You don't say the words *I think* in a courtroom. You don't say, "I think the room was painted blue." You say, "The room was painted blue."

While I was in law school, I skipped a lot of classes. I traveled continuously consulting in personal injury cases all over the country.

A woman moved into the condo next door. I saw her outside one evening, and we got talking and she said, "I'm retiring here. I was a legal secretary to the judge of the Court of Appeals who retired and now is teaching at the law school. You may meet him while you're in law school. When he retired, I retired."

"Would you work for me?" I asked.

"What do you mean?" she said.

"I dictate a lot, and if I give the tapes to you, you type them, then bring them to me and I'll pay you by the hour," I said.

"Oh that's wonderful," she said.

And so she became my secretary. She told her former boss, and he also became my friend. I was proud to be friends with a retired appeals court judge.

After a while my law professors understood that frequently I didn't show up in class because I was on the road helping at trials. I wasn't a lawyer as yet, but I was going to trials and advising on medical issues in big cases around the country.

One day the retired appellate judge and I were having coffee when he said that one of the professors was questioning how I could consult in trials around the country when I had not yet even graduated law school. He said he replied, "If you had been in court as often as Dr. Rein, maybe you could consult too." True, but that did not make the professor my friend and we always need all the friends we can make.

"Thanks a lot," I said to the judge. "That's going to make me a big hit with him."

Law school was easy. My photographic memory helped me remember what I needed to know and made it possible for me to enhance my consulting work. Even before I took the bar exam, a lawyer I knew, Neal Evans of Jacksonville, Florida called and asked if he could visit. He arrived in his car. His trunk and backseat were loaded with files which we carried into my home. Neal asked me to review and sort them. He wanted me to tell him which were of value for a lawsuit.

It took about a week to do and he was satisfied with the results. When a case of a doctor failing to properly diagnose and treat heart disease in a young person arose, he asked me to help him try the medical aspects of the case. I was flattered and worked hard. The trial came and I thought I performed admirably for my first Florida trial.

When the jury went to deliberate, the judge wrote a large settlement number on his desk pad, which he discussed with us. It was expected that the jury would be out several hours, and the judge told the defense lawyer, "You should settle the case, because you likely will be hit with a very large verdict."

Within 20 minutes the jury was back with a defense verdict. I was devastated. Having little experience, I had no understanding of how this could happen. Depressed, I felt that I needed to reconsider my future law career. Neal insisted that I had done a great job, that I had made and created my reputation in the Jacksonville area, and that even with this loss he and I would be able to settle cases easier because of the fear I had created in the defense by my work in this case.

I didn't believe him. I felt he was flattering me. He saw how depressed I was and behaved like a true friend. Before the month was out he called me and said that the same defense lawyer who had beaten me in this case offered about two times as much as we had decided we would be willing to take on another case being prepared for trial.

We accepted. And similar settlements happened again after that.

CHAPTER 15

PROTECTING PATIENTS

In 1984 I had my first really big case. It had to do with a product called Pitocin that is given intravenously during labor to induce contractions or to make them stronger. This, in turn, also increases the presuure on a baby's head and body, and risks decreasing the oxygen supply to the baby's brain. The child must be protected from that and usually medical staff will note changes in the fetal heart rate. This used to be done with a hand on the mother's belly during contractions, by listening with a fetoscope to the baby's heart, and then through electronic fetal monitoring. Timely intervention, if necessary, is essential to protect the baby from oxygen deprivation while it is in the uterus. In this case, the fetal monitor became abnormal and was not recognized by the doctor or the obstetric nurse and this beautiful child was born with cerebral palsy.

I needed an expert witness on Pitocin to prosecute my case on behalf of this baby and his parents.

Dr. Louis Hellman was chairman of the obstetric department at John Hopkins University Hospital in Baltimore. He introduced intravenous Pitocin into the United States and so besides being an obstetrics expert, he was the world's expert in the use of Pitocin. At the time the case was about to go to trial Dr. Hellman was working in Washington D.C. as Undersecretary of Health and Human Services. He was tasked with advising the government on women's health issues. Opposing me was one of the best defense lawyers in central Florida. I needed an expert on our side. I prayed Dr. Hellman would be my expert witness. I found out where he lived and called him. I told him I had once been one of his students.

"May I come up and visit with you? I have a Pitocin issue."

"Sure," he said. "I live in the Watergate complex."

"When can I come up?"

"Give me a few days' notice."

We arranged that Rhea and I would fly up to Washington for a little vacation the next week and also see Dr. Hellman. When he opened the door I could see he was shaking with Parkinson's. I told him about my Pitocin case.

"Pitocin never should have been used that way," he said after I'd briefed him on the case.

"I'm glad you agree with me, because that's what I really came for," I said. "Can you be the expert witness in the case?"

He said no.

"Why?" I asked.

"My boss, Casper Weinberger, would not approve of it," he said. "Everyone around here is concerned about the medical litigation crisis and I can't be an expert witness against a doctor. I shouldn't be an expert witness about anything, but certainly not against a doctor."

"Look at this brain damaged baby." I pulled out the pictures. "Look at him."

"I can't be an expert witness against a doctor," he repeated.

"Everything you taught me in medical school went wrong in this case because it was improperly handled by the physician, right?"

"I can't be a witness against a doctor," he again said and showed me the door. I was frustrated and felt let down. On the way out I muttered, "So I guess everything you taught us in medical school was bullshit?"

"You have a funny way of expressing yourself," Dr. Hellman said. Rhea was aghast my words. Dr. Hellman paused and said, "You know, I don't remember you at all."

"Really?" I said. "Let me tell you a story." And I recounted the story about him only giving me a C when I deserved an A. I quoted his line, "I won't change it because the residents resent you."

He stared at me. "I remember that conversation," he said, and then paused before saying, "I will help you."

And because Dr. Hellman was my expert witness, the case was settled quickly for a substantial amount of money to ensure the child received good medical care, lower extremity appliances as needed, and tutoring to maximize his learning ability.

The lesson I learned was to be nice to people but also be ready to push them to do the right thing. Dr. Hellman remains one of my heroes.

CHAPTER 16

SHAMING THE DEVIL

One of the largest cases I took part in occurred in the mid-1980s after a doctor failed to take action when fetal monitor strips showed the baby wasn't getting enough oxygen. The usual response is to form an emergency caesarean.

Monitor strips are recordings using an electrode placed on a woman's belly that records the baby's heartbeat on a strip of continuously running paper. If the baby is experiencing difficulty the strip shows this. But the doctor was in a hurry. He took a quick look at the strip the nurse brought to his attention and said, "Oh, they're okay. It's a minor issue." And then he went home and didn't come back until the morning.

During the night the monitor strip kept showing the same abnormalities. As the night wore on they became worse and when the baby was born, the doctor had to deliver in a hurry because when he walked in he recognized that the situation was urgent. He used forceps and didn't use them properly. The baby had a lot of marks on her face from the forceps. It upset the nurse and the mother, but that didn't cause the harm, because two days later the marks were gone. But it *was* a trigger. People thought the forceps caused the brain damage that led to the baby's later diagnosis of cerebral palsy. What caused the brain damage was hours of insufficient oxygen. The doctor should have gotten the baby out of there when the nurse first showed him the strip, but he didn't. He went home.

When the baby developed more overt signs of cerebral palsy as a child – she limped and had a learning disability – the parents sued the hospital and the doctor. In this case the nurse was a pleasant and gentle woman who cared, but not enough to risk her job. The arrogance of doctors and the supercilious way they sometimes treat nurses is often a major problem.

When the trial came, I glued all the monitoring strips together and made them into a roll that stretched out about thirty-five feet. On the way to the trial my wife said, "Be gentle with her," meaning the nurse, "If you attack her in your wolfhound way, the jury will hate you."

When my wife speaks, I listen. The nurse took the stand and I stood as far away from her as possible. When the time came for us to discuss the strips, I was almost at the other end of the courtroom. I spoke very slowly and quietly so that a hush came over the room. She expected that I would be rough on her. Instead, I was a pussycat. I asked her to look at the strips one page at a time. After an hour I asked, "Do you see the abnormalities?"

"Not yet," she said.

We scrolled onward.

"Go ahead and look again," I said. "Do you see the abnormalities now?"

"Not yet," she repeated.

"All right," I said, "go some more. Do you see the abnormality?"

"Well, just a little bit, but it's not significant," she said.

We kept going, and when I gently repeated my question, she was silent. I waited. It was quite a while as I allowed suspense to build.

"It's a little worse, isn't it?"

"Well, just a little," she said.

We went on like this for about twenty minutes, and again I asked, "It's worse, isn't it?"

Again she was quiet.

"Can you hear me?" I asked.

No answer.

"It's worse, isn't it," I repeated.

And then she started to cry.

"Oh my God," she said. "I should have called him."

Just like that, the trial was over. We went through the usual steps for the next three or four days, but at that point the fault of the doctor and hospital were recognized. The jury could see that they were all protecting themselves. No one was willing to admit anything. If I had been rough in my questioning, she could have said, "No, it's not abnormal," and experts would have lined up to say it wasn't abnormal enough to cause damage to the child. So how you approach a matter can often determine your success.

The disappearing witness

In another case I had a disappearing witness. It had to do with a back injury in the Bahamas. I was presenting the injury based on thermography; a printing technique in which a wet ink image is fused by heat or infrared radiation with a resinous powder to produce a raised impression. It's often used to detect tumors. The patient's Miami neurologist said, "I'll be happy to testify in this case and tell you what's wrong with her, and if it's confirmed by thermography, you should win."

"Tomorrow we'll be in Nassau," I said, "and if you fly down the night before, you can testify at 11a.m., and then fly home."

The plaintiff was a Nassau resident who came to Miami for medical care after a car accident in which she sustained a lower back injury. Thermography had been used to verify the diagnosis of the south Florida neurologist she consulted with. Such evidence is hard to contradict.

After I arrived in Nassau I ran into a local lawyer who said, "Hello, Harry. Nice to see you. What are you doing down here?"

He was part of the defense team, but I didn't know that.

"I'm here in a thermography case," I told him.

"Are you testifying?

"No," I said. "I'm the person who interpreted the thermograms."

"Do you know who the expert witness is?"

"The treating neurologist in Miami," I stupidly told him.

He quickly changed the subject.

"What are you going to do tonight?" he asked.

I said, "I'm going to have dinner, then go to my room and watch television."

But something about the conversation left me uneasy.

That evening my witness, the neurologist from Miami, didn't show up at the hotel. The next morning, I woke up and he had still not checked in.

I called the doctor at home and he was angry as a hornet. He had gotten on the airplane and arrived in Nassau. After checking into the hotel he called his wife to tell her everything was fine. But his wife was furious. An anonymous caller had phoned to say her husband was drinking, gambling, and womanizing.

After she excoriated him on the phone, he caught the next plane back to Miami, because his marriage was far more important to him than my case.

We told the judge that one of the defense lawyers was responsible for my witness not showing up in court. He denied it, of course.

"That's too bad," the judge said. "Things like that happen in the Bahamas. Case dismissed."

The Uncivil War

I was involved in another case in Kentucky, when I found I couldn't win because I was a Yankee and the judge was a good old boy from the

South. I was hired by a Louisville, Kentucky lawyer, Leonard Rosenberg who had a very big case in the Eastern Kentucky coal-mining district. It was an obstetrics case in which a woman carrying twins started bleeding in labor. The doctor didn't show up even though he was called several times. As a result, she and the twins died.

We represented the husband. It was a very simple case, because except in unusual circumstances, something like that rarely happens. The nurses testified that the attending physician drank a great deal and that in the past there were many times they had difficulty reaching him when they needed him. In this case they called him when the woman started bleeding and he didn't respond. They did the best they could.

We had evidence to show the hospital was being sued for allowing him to continue practicing after the nurses had reported multiple episodes of misconduct to the hospital.

About two months before the trial I got a call from Leonard Rosenberg. "Harry, I'm dropping out of this case," he said, "and you're welcome to take it over alone or hire somebody in Kentucky, but I don't want to have anything to do with it. I got a call from a lawyer in East Kentucky, who said, `Mr. Rosenberg, we know you're handling the case here in Eastern Kentucky. There was another Jew lawyer from your part of Kentucky one time, and he refused to take our advice, and one day he was just never heard from again. Let me tell you his name.'"

They gave Mr. Rosenberg his name. Rosenberg checked and sure enough, headlines blared that this lawyer had disappeared in Louisville, Kentucky.

Leonard said, "I'm too young to take a chance with this, so you can have the case."

I said, "Don't check out. Wait."

I made a few phone calls and let it be known that if Rosenberg left, I would hire one of the most famous personal injury lawyers in the country. So they offered Leonard Rosenberg a paltry $75,000 settlement for this $1-million-dollar case.

The husband said, "Take it. I'm going to put it out of my mind. It's gone on for two years. I need to get on with my life.

Leonard took it. And that was the end of the case.

Strep death

In another case, a woman went to a family doctor with a sore throat. The doctor considered strep throat, but he wrote it off because he was busy with an office full of patients. Because of his misdiagnosis, the woman's strep throat affected her heart and she died.

Before trial we took the doctor's deposition. I said to him, "You failed to do the correct thing because you just weren't careful enough, isn't that right?"

His lawyer could have intervened. He could have answered, "No, that's not right." Instead, the doctor just looked at me and said, "It's true." All that was left was a discussion of the settlement. Such conclusions are rare. But it has happened to me three times.

In another case I took the deposition of a kindly old doctor. I was told that everyone in the community loved him, so I knew bluster would work against me. Again I was gentle. I showed him some x-rays, which displayed evidence of a pulmonary embolism, a blood clot of the lung, which is something a doctor has to suspect if a patient develops a cough and chest pain a couple days after surgery. It may look like pneumonia, but you have to think blood clot. A pulmonary embolism has a high mortality rate.

I said to the doctor, "Do you see this x-ray?"

"Yes."

"You said it was pneumonia?"

"Yes.

"But it also looks like a possible pulmonary embolism, doesn't it?"

"Yes," he said.

"Did you consider pulmonary embolism that day?" I asked.

"No," he said, "because if I did, I would have put her right in the hospital."

"You should have considered it, shouldn't you have?" I asked.

"Yes," he said, "I should have."

Towards the end of the deposition I said, "Doctor, have you considered retiring?"

"No," he said, "but who knows?"

And the deposition ended.

Everybody left feeling that the case was going to settle, that it was just a question of what its fair value was. About five days later the defense lawyer called me, which is unusual. They usually call the named attorney on the case. The plaintiffs weren't my clients.

"I thought you'd be interested," said the defense attorney, "My client just called me and said he gave a lot of thought to your question in the deposition. He's retiring."

He was an older guy, and he just needed someone to tell him.

Guinea Pig

I started lecturing for the American Association of Gynecologic Laparoscopics near Washington D.C. in the early nineteen-eighties. On the first occasion, before I was due to speak, Rhea told me that there was a demonstration of the new laparoscopic instrument in the basement of the hotel. This is an instrument that you insert into the abdomen with a tiny incision and then observe inside the abdomen on a television screen while you manipulate the instrument. I had never done it before and I was never very good with it, though young doctors who played video games when they were children, were much more adept using it.

I went down to where they were demonstrating the instruments and I introduced myself. They asked if I'd like a demonstration, and I said, "I'd love it." A practice exercise was peeling an apple by watching the TV screen. "Just get the skin off the apple until it looks clean," I was told. I also was asked to burn my initials into an orange with the high-intensity tool without causing the orange to lose any juice. It requires excellent depth perception and a lot of practice. I destroyed several apples and I had a flow of juice coming out of my orange that made the instructor wince.

I then went to speak to the 600 doctors who were going to learn the procedure the next day. I told them, "Yesterday I went down to the basement of the hotel and played with the new instruments. Now I know that all of you will go there and you'll be amazed at what you see, and you'll learn how to use them. And when you are finished, you will go back to your offices and try to use them on your patients. I want to tell you that in two or three years from now, we may be seeing each other across the table in a lawsuit. When you've burned or cut someone while using those instruments without enough training, you may find me as a lawyer on the other side. So be very careful."

As it turned out, I was talking to deaf ears. No one wanted to hear it.

After I spoke an organizer said to me, "You were pretty rough on them. There is no reason to intimidate those who are here to learn."

"Somebody's got to tell them that two hours of training is not nearly enough," I said.

"That's the way it's done," he said.

"Well," I said, "what they learn in two hours is *not* good enough. There will be a lot of lawsuits, and I just thought I'd ring the bell and let them know."

"You rang the bell," he said.

Unfortunately, ringing the bell wasn't nearly enough. A woman with persistent stomach pain went to see a physician who told her, "You need to have your gall bladder removed."

"Okay," she said. "I'm tired of this ache. Let's set it up."

The doctor said, "Why don't you wait until next weekend? I'm taking a course in laparoscopic surgery for the gall bladder, and when I come back, I'll be an expert, and then I'll do it." She agreed.

At that time different doctors around the country taught the procedure in a $3,000 weekend course. The doctor learning the procedure would get a certificate written on parchment making him or her an 'expert.' Basically all that happened was that they watched videotape and handled some instruments. If they were lucky, they got to perform an operation on a guinea pig. The gall bladder is in the same location in a guinea pig as it is in a human. You can use the same instruments on a guinea pig. Operating on this small furry animal was part of this doctor's course. When he returned from his weekend seminar, he told his patient, "Now I'm an expert."

He may have thought he was an expert, but he wasn't. Over and over I would see cases like this where inadequately trained, over-confident doctors caused harm. In this case, during surgery the doctor cut the wrong duct and the patient had trouble that lasted for months. She had to have multiple surgical repairs.

I flew to Nashville where the doctor took the course. I introduced myself to the doctor trainers and asked if they would help me in a malpractice case as expert witnesses. They tried to throw me through the front door without opening it, until one of the doctors asked if I would like to learn how to do the procedure. I said I would.

"I'm going to show you how to do it in two hours, rather than the usual two days," he said. So I was taught how to do laparoscopic surgery for gall bladder removal in two hours. It wasn't enough to learn how to do the procedure properly, but at least I knew what the course was all about.

I went back and took the deposition of the doctor. He admitted that the course I had taken was the course he took. The defense didn't want the jury to know I had taken the same course as the doctor, because I too, was now supposedly an expert.

It's dishonest to do something that's more than what you really know how to do. He wasn't careful enough. It's always about being *careful enough* and caring.

I was so concerned that doctors were performing this surgery without enough training that I started lecturing on the issue. I was never sure how taking a weekend course in gall bladder surgery could make a doctor expert enough to operate. I became concerned that doctors were opening themselves up to malpractice suits by not exercising due care.

Laparoscopic malpractice cases became more common. I worked on the first five in Florida where doctors caused gall bladder surgical injury and I was a lawyer for the patients in every one of them. We got very good results for each.

The Cure

In another case, I had a psychiatric patient. He was educated, but used wild language, and was suicidal. He was in his late 20s when his family finally decided they needed to commit him. At that time in Florida anyone with good reason could have someone committed under the Baker Act by complaining to a physician or to law enforcement. The person would then be committed for three days.

This patient was committed to a local hospital, but the psychiatric section of the hospital was full, so they put him in a room on the third floor. He was sedated and the medical staff told him, "If you need anything, push this button and we'll come." Later that afternoon he opened the window to his room and jumped out. The hospital was lucky he didn't die. He broke both ankles and now has a disability. Oddly enough the pain from the ankles was so great it overshadowed the mental illness. But once the physical pain subsided it came back.

He sued and the hospital defended itself by saying it had cured his mental illness. However, the crux of the suit had to do with the hospital's obligation to protect patients, especially if it knows the patient is a danger to himself.

"This is not a malpractice case," I told the court. "It's a case about a hospital allowing this patient to leave through the wrong exit."

Loose lips

One of the serious problems patients face in their interactions with doctors is that if they ask too many questions some doctors won't want to treat them. I found this out one time when I was skiing at Jackson Hole, Wyoming. My son-in-law Ross and I walked out of the lodge where we were staying and I slipped on the ice, and broke my wrist.

We went to the nearby hospital. They took x-rays and determined my wrist was broken. The doctor said, "I think this can be set properly with a local anesthetic."

"Yes," I said, "I think so too. Have you ever done this before?"

This is one of the most intelligent questions a patient can ask, but patients are usually too cowed or ignorant to ask it.

"Why?" he asked.

"I'd like to know how many broken wrists you've set so I can decide whether to stay here or to fly into Salt Lake City or Denver to have it done."

"Are you a doctor?"

"Yes, I am," I said. I didn't tell him I was also a lawyer.

He said he had done perhaps fifty or sixty such operations.

"I suppose you're also a surgeon?" he asked.

"Yes," I said, "and I'm also a right-handed surgeon. Does that trouble you in fixing my right wrist?"

"No, "he said, "I will be even more careful."

"That's good," I said with a laugh. "I'm glad I mentioned it otherwise you'd be less careful."

"That's not what I meant," he said.

I decided to let him operate. A male nurse gave me an IV for anesthesia for my upper extremities. They didn't have any anesthesiologists.

"Have you done any of these before?" I asked him.

"Sure," he said, "I've done this lots of times."

"Do you know how to manage a cardiac arrest?" I asked.

"Why?"

"Sometimes the medication causes cardiac arrest," I said, "and if it's me having the cardiac arrest, I want you to know how to manage it. Do you know how?"

He looked at me weirdly, but the doctor said, "I do. I'm an EMT. Don't worry, it's not going to happen."

The nurse then asked me to take my shirt off. And my trousers.

"Why my trousers?" I asked.

"Because that's what we do here," he said.

"Where are you putting the IV?" I asked.

"Your arm."

"Are you going to put any in my groin?"

"No."

"So why do you want me to take my pants off?"

"Because it's the routine around here."

"I've only been here thirty minutes," I said to the nurse, "but you have to know by now that I don't do routine. If you can give me one good reason to take my pants off, I will. Otherwise, they are staying on."

"Let him leave his pants on, please," the doctor said.

The risk of routine

Ritual and routine is often done without any thought. There's a great commercial on TV showing a young woman texting. The narrator says, "Five seconds is all she took her eyes off the road." And then it shows how far she was able to travel in five seconds before she ran through a red light and was hit by a truck. Texting is why driving today is much more dangerous than it used to be.

The trouble with ritual and routine is that you think a little less. And that's when you get in trouble. In medicine no two cases are exactly alike. Every case has to be treated individually. *You have to do the right thing at the right time in the right way for the right reason.* If you don't get the expected result, you need to find out why you didn't get the expected result and then take steps to correct that.

There are times when you routinely run lab tests, and if you don't get the expected results, you have to find out why. If there is an abnormal return, you can't just say, "I just did this routine test because we always do it."

If you don't pay attention to the abnormality, it may well come back and bite you. Thus you had better know what you're doing and why. Doing that can prevent so many malpractice cases. Don't do the wrong thing at the wrong time in the wrong way for the wrong reason – ever. Any one of those may lead you down the path of no return.

A very athletic woman in her 40s fell off her bicycle and injured her wrist. It hurt badly and so she went to the hospital and was treated by a local doctor. Even though she was in great pain, the doctor told her nothing was broken.

She went to a wrist orthopedist.

"You have some ligament damage," he said. "We better do arthroscopy. We can clean up the ligaments, and then we'll put you in a splint. You'll be in the splint six weeks and then we'll have therapy and see how it does."

She had the surgery. Six weeks went by. She was out of town, and it was time for an x-ray and the splint to be removed. She worked near a medical clinic and so she went there and told the doctor, "I'm supposed to have an x-ray to see if I can take the splint off." They took an x-ray and discovered a tiny circular piece of metal in the area inside the wrist where she had the arthroscopy.

"What is it?" she asked.

"I don't know," said the doctor.

"May I take my x-rays back to my surgeon?"

She went to see the surgeon. She brought a friend as a witness.

"I have no idea what that piece of metal is," he said. "It looks like the back of a stud earring."

"I wasn't wearing earrings," she said, "and I don't think you were. Was anyone wearing an earring that might have fallen in?"

"No," he said.

"Well, what do you think it is?" she wanted to know.

"I have no idea," he said, "but maybe it came from a previous surgery." He was making up an answer.

"A previous surgery?" she said.

He looked at her record and said, "Well, you had surgery on your shoulder and they put in a couple of screws."

"That was fifteen years ago," she said, "and it was the other shoulder."

"Well, it can travel in strange ways," he said.

She thought, *now he's treating me like a fool.*

"I want it out," she said.

"You don't really need to take it out," the doctor said.

"I want it out," she insisted.

When they took it out, it turned out to be the tip of one of the instruments that he had used in the operation. It wasn't supposed to come off, but it did. The doctor didn't see it come off. This smart lady had all her x-rays looked at by another doctor and it turned out that her doctor also missed two joint injuries that should have been repaired when he was doing the surgery.

The instrument manufacturer was sued and questioned. They couldn't understand how the tip came off.

"When it came off," the rep said, "the doctor should have seen that it came off."

The doctor should have noticed that he wasn't completing the task with the entire instrument. Most people are good people and can handle the unvarnished truth when it's explained to them. The doctor should have said, "I don't know what happened. It has never happened before, but I can and will fix it."

That's all it takes.

The case has not gone to trial yet. The doctor is arguing she doesn't have any significant damages and that the operation to take out the tip didn't lead to any permanent disability of any kind. Be that as it may, I don't think the jury is going to like hearing about how the doctor made up the story about how the tip of his instrument traveled from one arm to the other. The jury could penalize him for that and increase her damages.

Why did he feel he had to lie to her? Why didn't he just tell her the truth?

The answer: Unbelievable ego, which gets people in trouble over and over again.

CHAPTER 17

THE JUDICIARY

I am an inveterate gate-crasher. Curiosity has led me into more rooms and surgeries than I can recall and often it has resulted in life-changing outcomes. In 1989, I was in Washington, D.C. to be inducted into the Supreme Court. It coincided with an American Trial Lawyers Association meeting. There was a lull in proceedings and so I wandered around the conference center and entered a room in which there was a long conference table. Eight or nine people were seated at one end and so I sat down at the other end. They looked at me strangely, and after about half an hour, one of them asked, "Who are you?"

"I am a spy," I joked.

They looked at me curiously and didn't say anything.

It turned out they were all senior judges. The meeting was being held under the auspices of the American Inns of Court, a national organization run by judges to teach ethics and to mentor legal practitioners and theorists about justice, propriety and fairness.

I sat through the meeting and when it was over, I left, and came back the next day. Again I sat at the far end of the conference table by myself, and as one of them was talking, in my mind I disagreed with him, and I guess I started shaking my head.

One of the men said to me, "It seems like you disagree with what we are saying. Why don't you come and sit closer?"

I did, they inquired of me, and I explained why I disagreed. The meeting continued.

One of those in the meeting asked me what I was doing in Washington, D.C. and I told him. He suggested I join the group for dinner that night at the Supreme Court. He was Judge Paul Cotter, chief judge of the Nuclear Regulatory Commission.

At that dinner I found out more about The Inns of Court. They were initially established in England in the mid-13th century to promote wider understanding of the law and its ethical use. Seven centuries later, in the 1970's, Chief Justice of the United States Warren E. Burger and Judge J. Clifford Wallace of the U.S. Court of Appeals for the Ninth Circuit were discussing how to improve legal practice here. They liked the dignity and authority of Britain's ancient Inns of Court and wanted to emulate it here. Burger invited Rex E. Lee, then Dean of the J. Reuben Clark School of Law at Brigham Young University and later U.S. Solicitor General, and Dallin Oaks, then president of Brigham Young University and later justice of the Utah Supreme Court, to test the idea.

Lee suggested a pilot program be entrusted to Senior U.S. District Court Judge A. Sherman Christensen. He and Chief Justice Burger had been impressed, while in China too, that no matter how tense the battle between legal minds both sides would always be exceedingly polite. These two noble justices recognized that good things can come out of education, direction, expectations, and mentoring. The first American Inn of Court was founded February 2, 1980 in the Provo/Salt Lake City area of Utah, and included law students from Brigham Young University. Over the next three years, additional American Inns formed in Utah, Mississippi, Hawaii, New York, and Washington, D.C.

The men in the meeting I'd gate-crashed were members of the Washington D.C. Inns of Court and part of the national leadership. At dinner I had a conversation with Justice William Kennedy and found him to be absolutely brilliant. He knew more about everything that had to do with law than anyone I had ever spoken to. I was very interested in the Constitution and how it should be interpreted, because it's the fundamental basis of all the law and all the freedoms we have in the United States. I am fascinated by the arguments between the founders, particularly between James Madison and Alexander Hamilton, who wrote the Federalist Papers.

Justice Kennedy was an expert in this field. I was awed. The next day I was sworn in to the Supreme Court along with a dozen others, and afterwards it was announced that Justice Kennedy would be lecturing to everyone in the room on the Constitution.

He started speaking. I don't know how much time went by, but I suddenly had a very severe pain in my left rib cage, I soon realized it was my wife's sharp elbow, because I had fallen asleep during the presentation of the most brilliant man I had met that weekend.

Meeting Judge Cotter was one of those life-changing good fortunes I experienced more than once. "I'm looking for someone like you," he said. "How would you like me to appoint you as a part-time judge on the Nuclear Regulatory Commission?"

"I would be delighted," I said.

"But you don't even know what the job is," Judge Cooper said.

"You don't know how much I always wanted to be a judge," I said.

And he appointed me. All because I was curious and decided to sit in on a meeting. I had to fill out a form to get a security clearance and I listed the names of people as references. They never interviewed them, but they did go across the street from our house in Orlando and knocked on the door of our neighbors. It was Passover, and my neighbor had a full house of visitors when the FBI agents came knocking on her door. She liked to keep her shades drawn and she always kept a chain on the front door.

When the FBI knocked on the door, she opened it slightly and said, "Yes?"

"We are from the FBI. We want to ask you a few questions about Dr. Rein."

"I'm not talking to you," she said and slammed the door in their faces.

Later she came to see me.

"Two guys saying they were FBI agents came to my door," she said, "they asked about you. I slammed the door in their faces. Just because they had badges, I wasn't going to tell them anything. I looked through the blinds and I could see them sitting in their car. An hour later I looked and they were still sitting there. So I thought maybe they really are from the FBI. I went out and told them they could come in. They said they were investigating you, because you want to be a judge in Washington.

"I told them, `Oh, he's wonderful.' They were so happy to see that I knew you, and they left. I was so rude to them at first, I hope I didn't ruin your career."

The FBI also interviewed one of the senior members of the Inns of Court. He said they asked whether I drink and if I gamble. He said that he had never even seen me have a cocktail at the Inns of Court gathering and as far as he knew I didn't gamble.

"He has so much money that he doesn't need any more," he told them. They left. I got top secret civilian clearance from the FBI and so I became a judge, if only part-time. The power that comes from being a judge is unbelievable. It opens a lot of doors, but it has to be very carefully used. In 1990, I started the First Inn of Court of Central Florida, and we now have several Inns of Court in Central Florida, I am the founding father of all of them.

First case

I was made a judge on Thursday July 16, 2015 and my first assignment came shortly after appointment. It related to a major litigation in northern New York state where during a routine check, a plant operator was found using marijuana on the job. A particularly smart woman technician noted that when she was given the urine sample it was cold and not warm as one would expect. Upon investigation it was found that the man who gave the specimen kept clean urine in a thermos bottle in his locker and this is what he used when inspections were made. This resulted in the Nuclear Regulatory Commission changing their contract with the plant. The plant objected and a trial was held. I was one of three judges appointed, because it was a medical issue.

My wife came along as my judicial assistant. On the first day, the courtroom was filled with spectators and media. Sadly, no one appeared to be ready and after an hour and a half of hemming and hawing I could not restrain myself and asked why no one was ready. I pointed out that they were being paid by the hour and and the expense of the judges and their assistants traveling to Syracuse would be born by the taxpayer of the United States. I asked, "Am I the only one that cares?" The newspaper reporters were writing like crazy. The meeting was adjourned for thirty days for work to be completed that could be done in two hours.

The senior judge took me aside and said my frankness was not the way it was done in Washington or by the Nuclear Regulatory Commission. This was to be followed by many episodes where I would intervene using my knowledge, skills and new power over the next twelve years and it often led to admonishment by senior judges.

In another trial the issue was about an improper signature on an application in which the applicant is sworn to tell the truth. This involved a doctor applying to use radioactive iodine for medical purposed with N.R.C. approval. The doctor lied about his training. After three days of hearings I could no longer restrain myself and looked at him and asked if he knew I was a physician even though I was also a judge.

I looked him directly in the eye and said, "You are just sitting here and lying to us aren't you?"

There was a stunned silence in the room.

His answer was simply, "Yes."

The case ended as it should have two and a half days earlier. The people in that jurisdiction are safer without a dishonest physician in their midst.

CHAPTER 18

THE TORAH BRINGS HEALING

My parents always refused to go back to Austria, the memories were too painful, both had lost their parents and relatives. Neither knew what had become of their mothers. They were not only traumatized by their experiences and of those they knew, but they had survivor's guilt, and in some ways all of that sadness, though less, gets passed on.

In 1970, when Robin was 13 and Debra was 11, Rhea and I decided to go to Vienna and revisit the sites my parents had spoken of.

After our plane landed in Vienna, the first place I went to see was the apartment I lived in when I was a child. I stopped our car at the address. There it was. It had a plaque that said it had been damaged by an American aircraft, but had been restored. This was where I was born. This was where I lived as a child.

Diagonally across the street was the apartment house where my grandmother lived on the third floor with the grocery store on the ground floor. I told my children about how I used to go in there, and how the shopkeeper used to give me a piece of candy. "Wait here," I said to them. "I'm going to go in and find out what they can tell me about my grandmother, Mrs. Drucker. Maybe someone remembers her."

I walked into the grocery store. Inside was the shopkeeper, he was an older man. I waited while a couple of women made purchases, and when everyone had left the store, I said to the shopkeeper in broken

German, "Guten morgen. My name is Doktor Rein. Have you been here a long time?"

He laughed and said, "Ja. I've been here a long time. I was working here as a young man."

"I want to inquire about my grandmother," I said. "She lived on the third floor. Her name was Drucker. Do you know what happened to her?"

I felt the air chill. He looked at me and said, "We have nothing to talk about."

I asked another question, but he just stared at me. I felt a strange fright and anger. I had money, I had power, I was a professional, and there was nothing to be afraid of. But, emotions cause strange reactions.

We know from the Red Cross that my grandmother had left and perhaps been made to go on a forced march to Belgium. When and where she died will never be known.

I walked out of the store and got back into the car. When my wife and daughters asked what had happened, I said, "We'll talk about it later."

We drove back to the hotel, and I said, "Pack our bags." We drove to the airport. I turned in our car and we left Austria, not to return for many years.

At that time nothing in Vienna had been cleaned. All the buildings were covered in soot so everything was grey. Now my mind was grey. My soul was grey.

We flew to Dublin, which became one of my favorite cities. I thought that I never again would return to Vienna. Finally, we understood why my parents wouldn't go back and why they wouldn't let me take them back to visit.

Seventy-six years after I left Austria, and after many subsequent visits to a happier, cleaner and modernized Vienna, my personal story seemed to come full circle.

At the same time, I was fleeing Austria with my family in 1938, a man by the name of Goldschmidt was living in the city of Berkach, Germany. The Nazis decided that Germany should be free of Jews, and began throwing us out, or incarcerating us, or burning us in ovens. At the same time the Nazis were burning synagogues, and doing all they could to harass Jews. Mr. Goldschmidt took a torah, a holy scroll representing the soul of the Jewish people, from a synagogue and ran off with it. When he and his family arrived at Ellis Island, his name was changed to Gould, and later his family including a son Lothar arrived in Orlando.

By chance, or if there is a celestial design, the Gould's and I ended up in the same synagogue -- Temple Israel, Orlando Florida. Many years later I got to know them when I became the synagogue president. The elderly Mr. Gould died and the son, who was somewhat older than me, told members of the congregation the story of the old torah that his father had rescued from the Nazis during the Holocaust.

It was kept in the synagogue, but could not be used because it was damaged and torn. Some of the manuscript had been worn off and letters were missing. Years went by, and in 2010 the synagogue decided to raise funds to repair the torah and use it as a reminder and historic link. Restoration would cost about $20,000. We had to hire a special scribe.

Before we did that, we contacted the synagogue in the city of Berkach to verify the story Mr. Gould had told was true. Some of the parishioners didn't want us to do that for fear that Berkach would want their torah back.

In the meantime, I had the responsibility of negotiating with the scribe, and getting him to come to Orlando to work on it. He repaired the torah one letter at a time, and pieced it back to together until it once again as new and religiously pure and usable.

As one of the contributors to this project, Rhea and I were given the honor of writing in the first letter of the first word, which is *Brei-sheet (In the beginning....).*

Early in 2014, we were called by one of the Berkach townspeople and told that the synagogue that our newly repaired torah had come from still existed. It was covered with weeds, in poor repair, and one person, a non-Jew, was working to clean and recondition it. Berkach was a town of only 300 people. No Jews were living there. All had either fled or been killed in the gas chambers.

The town's representative said, "We want to rededicate the synagogue and make it a community event. May we borrow the torah?"

Rhea and I and two others flew to Germany for this great honor and memorial event. We did face one problem: getting the torah on the airplane. It could not be treated as baggage nor checked in the usual manner. On the way over, due to the grace of Delta, the Torah had its own seat and was strapped in. But on the return flight, I was responsible and did not have that luxury. As I attempted to carry it onto the plane properly protected and boxed, they wouldn't let me on because it was five-feet high and a foot square in a special box made for it. I let the flight attendant know it was a priceless religious object that we couldn't possibly check.

"It must come on board," I said. And they said no.

Maybe what had worked in China thirty years earlier would succeed again.

"It's very, very expensive, and you don't want to be responsible for it," I said.

"What do you call expensive?" I was asked in German.

"Maybe 350,000 euro," I said.

"We'll take special, special care of it," she said, and she stood it very carefully in the forward closets in the plane. An hour later she came over to me and said, "I checked it, and it's safe and exactly where we put it."

I was very appreciative.

When we arrived in Berkach, just about every important politician in that section of Germany came for the ceremonies. The secretary-general came, as did local governors and mayors, the attorney general of the area, along with a lot of the local people. Only one Jew attended from the town of Berkach – a man who was converting to Judaism, a man who was very proud of the synagogue and proud that we had brought the torah back to its former home.

What was startling was that many of the people who came to the event were in their 80s. None were Jews. They were the Germans who had stood by silently and watched the Jews be taken away and gassed.

They got up and told stories of what they remembered from the 1930s when they were children. They said they couldn't understand why they did the terrible things they were told to do, how it was okay to insult the Jews, to spit on them, to break windows, trash their homes and possessions, and insult them. And as the war went on, one after the other said, they had horrible guilt feelings about what they had done, and it was only now, at this event, that they were able to tell their story. As each one stood there and spoke, these older people cried.

A dozen high school students read from diaries that had been hidden by frightened German townspeople who feared the Nazis. These words had been hidden over seventy years. They read of the fear and of the shame. As they read, silence came over the community, and it was as if the ground trembled.

For me, it was a reminder of the angel on my shoulder, of how strangely lucky we had been to escape the Holocaust, when so many of my relatives had died.

LIFE'S LESSONS

These are the lessons you learn from people: all they want is to be treated fairly, honestly, and with respect, they don't want anything else. They don't want *things*. What people want from us more than anything else is just to be treated nicely. You think when you buy a gift, you've done your thing, when all they want is for you to listen and to not give them advice before they're finished talking.

I have learned from my patients that in the first part of conversation they are just venting. Listening skills are natural for beauticians and manicurists. Those people know how to listen. People will tell a beautician or manicurist things they wouldn't say to their closest family members. You know why? Because that person is ready to listen and not judge. It's a trick everyone should learn. Many doctors and lawyers don't; but they should do the same.

Lessons in Attitude

In my early trial work, I had a mentor, T.G. LaGrone, and although I was older than he, his legal experience predated mine by almost two decades. He was perfecting legal procedure and trial tactics while I was perfecting sutures and a good bedside manner. He did not give up easily and when teaching as a guest lecturer at my seminars, he would say, "You will lose all your bad cases. You lose many of your good cases, and you will either lose some of your great cases; but when you win, how good it feels."

I've adapted football Coach Lou Holtz' tips for players because all patients and clients have worries, fears, and think of the same questions when they hire professionals. They wonder:

Are you committed to excellence, and will you do the best you can? Will you take time to think about my problem? Study if needed. And, treat me as you would like to be treated?

Trust

Trust is the glue that holds families together. It encourages strangers to allow you to do more. It does not just happen, it does not simply result from requests, nor can it be demanded or expected. Trust is a catalyst that makes things work. It is the enzyme that promotes unity. In the professional world, trust raises the quality of work, stimulates extra effort and creates initiatives where such may have been dormant or buried under mountains of required production. Trust is an expectation that wants to be fulfilled. Trust is a self-replenishing fuel. I have learned from all my "angels" that they provide opportunity but do not do the work. I believe that they watch and then smile a little as we take advantage of the path they have laid before us.

Challenging Authority

Challenging authority must be accompanied by an offer of service or recommendation that is likely acceptable by the person in control. Challenging authority requires having a better idea, the expectation and willingness to work harder, and at the same time crediting the challenged authority with the inspiration to dare to be better.

Learn How to Walk Away

By 1989, I was a large investor in the largest privately held mortgage company in Central Florida, when a financial bubble burst. The two principal owners of the company were running what seemed like a Ponzi scheme, and after one of the other investors lodged a complaint with the authorities, the two women in charge were arrested and convicted, and the mortgage company was seized. Since I was the primary investor, I took it upon myself to manage my family holdings in the business. I was determined to rescue the bad mortgages, find the fraudulent investments, and be certain the debtors knew what had happened, letting them know that we – the owners of the paper - were the new creditors.

I personally visited the properties trying to collect money. One day my father-in-law visited. I took Leon for a ride with me on one of my collection routes. It didn't take him long to understand the pressure I felt as I walked unsafe neighborhoods knocking on doors to collect from my borrowers. Leon asked if I was short on money, I told him I had lost a lot of money but that I was okay with money. I said I wasn't willing to walk away from the money others had defrauded from me.

His answer was profound. "I've been in business all my life," Leon said. "Every business has profits and losses, and I learned early to tally my profits and losses at the end of the year. If I had a loss, I tried to figure out what caused it and not to repeat the same mistake. I would start the New Year fresh. I never let past experiences interfere with my emotional state. It's all part of being in business, you win some, you lose some. In the long run you will come out ahead. Most important: Be happy."

My attitude changed. I became calmer and made some better financial and real property decisions.

The Doctor Who Loved His Patients

In 1989, I was reminded of how wonderful being a doctor once was after a chance meeting with a doctor from North Africa while I was visiting the southern African nation of Zimbabwe. Doctors from the American Academy of Gynecologic Laparoscopists, was invited to Zimbabwe to bring laparoscopic equipment and teaching techniques to physicians in small hospitals in Africa. I was asked if I would like to accompany the group to lecture on the U.S. legal system and how our experience might benefit newly democratic African countries. Zimbabwe had gained independence from white rule nine years earlier.

During our trip, surgeons taught laparoscopic techniques to physicians from all over Africa. The lectures were held in Harare, Zimbabwe. President Mugabe was in his first term of office, and he was converting the whole country, which for a century was ruled by English whites, into black rule. I could feel the tension between the races in the streets and in the restaurants. The seminars went very well. Most of the African doctors were awed by what they learned. Laparoscopic instruments every year were becoming more functional and smaller, and the instruments we were bringing these doctors were older models no longer in use in America. Even so, they were functional and badly needed by Africa's doctors, who were thrilled at the chance to get them.

There was one doctor at the back of the room, who I noticed hardly participated in the program. He had come from North Africa. I wondered whether the information he was getting was over his head. Toward the end of the stay I decided to approach him and ask him about his experience attending the clinic. He thanked me for coming and bringing our knowledge to his community, but then he began to cry, real tears. His tears came so fast and furious that he couldn't stop.

After he composed himself he explained that he came from a very small community, that he lived in a one-room house with no medical facilities. His kitchen was his medical office. His dining room table served as his examining table. He said he had a mattress that he put on top of the table when he had to give a patient an examination.

Through his tears he told me he had come to learn, but how could he possibly perform these procedures, which were common in the United States, when the nearest hospital was seventy-five miles away through the bush? His tears were the result of how much he cared for his patients and how great his frustration was at not being able to do very much to help them.

We had assumed when we came to Africa that all the doctors would accept all we were bringing them. Not this man. He said he couldn't and he wouldn't, but only because he had no capacity for practicing modern medicine. As he was saying this, I realized just how much he cared for his patients and how they were getting so much more one-on-one attention than patients in the United States now got from their doctors. I thought it ironic that while patient and doctor one-on-one care has been disappearing from the practice of medicine in the United States as a result of government intervention, insurance forms which need to be filled out, the fear of medical malpractice, and the administrative worry that exists in every medical office, this man loved his patients so much he wept because he could not give them all he believed they deserved. What a lesson.

"I envy you," I told him, and explained to him that the type of medicine he described was that which I had dreamed about before and during medical school. I told him he was practicing the kind of medicine that all current, true medical practitioners would envy.

"I so admire the way you manage your patients," I said. "Your concern for them is so admirable, and you are filling needs that no one but you can do."

I spoke from the bottom of my heart. I was hoping he appreciated my sentiments.

Several months later I received a letter from him saying how warm he felt toward me, and how my praise had raised his spirits with regard to his practice. He said that when he returned to his town to practice, he realized how much his patients respected him, admired him, needed him, and even loved him. He said that he realized that his patients trusted him completely, and that he was leading a wonderful life.

ADDENDUM

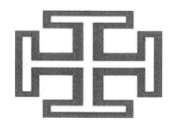

[Crutch Cross of Austria]

YES!

with Schuschnigg for a Free Austria

[Popular Slogan before the Nazis invaded Austria]

REMEMBERING DAYS OF
HORROR
A Fate of Hundred Thousands

PART I

On March 8, 1938 in Austria, then called the "Ostmark"- there was an agitated feeling and nervousness in the air with the general public, especially in Vienna, where I was born and in the country as such, that, at that time, I still considered to be my homeland. The following Sunday, general elections of the "Volk" were to take place, a so-called national referendum, to assess the present trust for the government in place, the government of S C H U S C H N I G G, which existed since the assassination of the prior Chancellor Dr. D O L L F U S S. As is known, Dr. Dollfuss was assassinated in the Chancellery on July 15, 1934[2] by the German National Socialist Party[3]. On this day was the great Coup by the Nazis that was, however, suppressed. After that day also 2 security organizations were founded. The "Homeland Security" ["Heimatschutz"] and the "Fatherland Front" ["Vaterland Front"]. They were founded as security for the general population and to prevent such happenings from recurring. However, unfortunately, in the next four years, the victims of these two organizations were only the socialists and the Jews and not the actual agitators for which they were founded. Wherever possible, the former were suppressed and their rights were taken away by order of the government of Schuschnigg. Under such circumstances it was, of course, easily understood that the

2 According to the Encyclopedia Britannica, the assassination of Engelbert Dollfuss happened on July 25, 1934

3 Nazi - National Socialist German Workers' Party

Nazis who were still illegal at the time, could secretly grow in importance, and showed themselves on a daily basis by many terror attacks and assassinations. This was going too far and it was without question that something had to be done to protect the country with all might in order not to be confronted suddenly by a catastrophe – which, however, occurred anyhow. Above all it was attempted to "strengthen" the governing party, The "Fatherland Front". Actually, this was the only official party that existed, since all other parties and associations were not allowed. Everyone had to join this party, whether he was willing or not, whether he supported this ideology or not; it did not matter – otherwise he was accused of high treason. A deadline to become a member of this party was determined as November 1, 1937. Anyone who had not declared his loyalty to this party by then could not be certain of his freedom. Therefore, I also had to submit to this regulation and destroyed my I.D. card for the S.D.A.P., Social-Democratic Labor Party and on October 25, 1937, I joined as member of the V.F., Fatherland Front.

In such times of disorientation and agitation as well as constant new compulsory regulations, days went by – weeks – and months.

The political arena became more tense and agitated, the climax was reached on March 8, 1938, when our Chancellor, Dr. Schuschnigg was supposed to hold a speech. All of Austria was in feverish expectation, of course also I and my family, and we sat around the loudspeaker and waited for a great surprise, for a final solution for the preservation of A u s t r i a and a declaration and assurance that the Socialist Labor Party is to obtain its rights back that were taken from it for the protection of the country. Finally, at ten after 8:00 o'clock our apprehensive waiting around the loudspeaker was over, when the voice of our Chancellor was heard. He spoke in a very large hall in Innsbruck before just as large a crowd. The end result of this one-hour speech was the following surprise:

Chancellor Schuschnigg announced that a referendum by the people was to be held at the following Sunday which I already mentioned before. This referendum by the people was to show confidence for the government and against the Nazis who were in uproar and enraged. The speech ended with the grandiose parole of the Chancellor and stormy ovations of the audience by his proclamation, shouted by his voice that was already hoarse: "Red-White-Red[4] until Death".

The following morning, walls were painted with this slogan, businesses and homes had their flags out – Red-White-Red – to show their approval and trust, road cobblestones and sidewalks were painted with glossy red and white paint proclaiming the same paroles, as well as with "Heil Schuschnigg". "Long live the Fatherland Front", they also portrayed large Krückenkreuze,[5]

in the colors of red-white-red. Everything was prepared for the coming referendum. By the way, this cost large amounts of money for the propaganda efforts in favor of the Schuschnigg government. No money should be spared for this occasion. Therefore, also the rich Jewish part of the population collected and provided the sum of 500,000 Austrian Shillings; they chose 3 delegates from the Vienna Israelite Religious Community to personally deliver the monies to Chancellor Schuschnigg with hearty well wishes. Although this government at that time had not much to spare for the Jewish population, the Jews still collected the monies since they wanted to choose the smaller one of two evils and to prevent from letting the N. S. D. A. P. (Nazis) get the upper hand. But, oh no, not even 48 hours later we had to listen to the voice of the Chancellor again with a short speech in which he declared his resignation and with a nearly sobbing voice (why this voice,

---

4 The colors of the Austrian flag.

5 Crutch crosses

to this day is a mystery to me), he spoke loud and clear and said: "God protect Austria".

At that moment all of us listening to the loudspeaker had tears in our eyes, perhaps not because Dr. Schuschnigg resigned but because we all knew – we were 8 people in the room – since our apartment neighbors were also present to hear the speech that was addressed to the "Austrian Volk" – what we had to expect, that means with other words, that now, our sad fate was finally sealed.

In his place, Dr. Seyss-Inquart became Chancellor who was a Nazi and who had been appointed to serve the government as Minister of the Interior a few weeks earlier; now with the sudden change in government over night, he became Chancellor, probably due to Hitler's demands of February 1938. Several minutes later – on the 12th of March 1938 at 6:00 in the evening, the new Chancellor announced on the radio that the German troops were on their way from the 3rd Reich and were already marching into Austria – and he pleaded with the Austrian population not to put up any resistance, what kind whatsoever; first of all, because it is useless and secondly, to avoid bloodshed. He repeated this plea on the radio every fifteen minutes since he feared that the Austrian workers would not let it pass them by without resistance. But, unfortunately, they were totally disarmed and their overall structure was totally fragmented with respect to what had been the ideology of the governments of Chancellors Dollfussβ and, later, Schuschnigg. Surprisingly, when the German forces moved across the Austrian borders into the provinces, they were greeted by large crowds with jubilation and songs. They shouted "Heil Hitler" with much gusto! Now everybody asked the question: What on earth happened to the Fatherland-loving followers? Where were the loyal Austrian soldiers for the defense of the Austrian independence? Where did the Fatherland protectors wander off or disappear to? Where were the 100,000 enthusiastic shouters who proclaimed "Red-White-Red until Death" only days ago? Everything had changed –

no sign of any of them. Loyalty changed overnight. Patriotism disappeared from the hearts of all – the true soul showed itself – unless, were almost all of them Fatherland fraudsters instead of Homeland protectors? Now they shouted again with utmost force: "Heil Hitler"!

Thus, Hitler and his followers marched through the provinces and cities of Austria. On the next day, the 13th of March, it was a Saturday; he concentrated his troops and led them into the capital, Vienna, arriving in the center of the city even by noon. But since he was not quite sure yet about his forces marching into Vienna – questioning whether everything would be as easy as into the other cities, to intimidate the 'Volk', he sent 200 airplanes that crossed over the city for 2 hours at very low altitude and created such a spectacle in order to scare the population. Finally, after this spectacle, the German military forces entered the city with a great parade, song and whistling. There were no more or no less than 300,000 solders. Schools and municipal buildings had to be vacated to house the military. All of this festivity did not last very long and soon enough "friendly" campaigns started.

Above all, the Austrian National Bank was robbed of its monetary inventory in gold, which was immediately transported by truck to Berlin; the next victims were grocery stores. Colossal transports of groceries were transported away, mostly to Germany because Germany was pretty much starving by then; and furthermore to feed the troops. Of course, the foodstuff was only taken from J e w I s h business people.

With the occupation of almost all important buildings by the German troops only their military campaign, their actual invasion ended, but their actual "raid" had just begun. All Austrian Nazis promptly got their uniforms and weapons, even if they had not reached their 18th year of age. Thus you saw youth running around on the street with weapons who acted importantly whose "snot was still running from their noses." They had now become our guardians to bring order in the chaos. Now they had a job to do.

All cars of Jewish owners were "acquired." Jewish major business people were arrested; at very first, those who had spent monies for the anticipated referendum for the Schuschnigg government; all Jewish municipal institutions and buildings were vacated and destroyed and in their place, horse stables, living quarters and barracks were built. Jewish temples were destroyed the prayer books and Torah were piled up to large heaps and burnt – all Jewish shops were plundered to the last nail – larger businesses were immediately transferred to Arian hands, the owner himself arrested and taken to a concentration camp; smaller businesses stayed on for a while and were still held by their owners; but they had smaller inventories than before, since the rest was lost to plunderers. Later on, the front of any Jewish shop was sentineled, not letting any Arian customer enter the store. Every passer-by was stopped to show his I.D. and was asked whether he was Jewish. If so, he would have to position himself in front of the store, holding a big board – stand at attention, without moving – and the board would read: "Don't buy anything from this Jewish Pig".

It did not matter whether you were old or young, rich or poor, sick or healthy, every Jew had to suffer and be bullied, even if it were by a 15-year old boy. The streets now had to be cleaned off the slogans that had been painted by the Fatherland Front, using glossy paint. In doing so, you could not use any sort of chemicals, like turpentine, lye or gasoline. You could only use clear water and a brush and, possibly, your fingernails. I need not mention that it was impossible to remove the slogans. The guards did not even care if the blood spritzed from your fingers. That's probably what they were waiting for. Jews had to clean the rooms in the barracks, clean bathrooms from the worst dirt – clean windows; only the most dangerous windows at certain heights or windows that were difficult to clean were assigned to us – also, washing cars and after the work was done, many were forced to swallow the soap that was left over – or if you refused to do so, you were beaten by the aggressors without looking at you. On the street, Jews were gathered up and transported in extra-large cars and trucks, like cattle, to different places for the purpose of cleaning jobs. Unfortunately, a lot of them never returned from these places to their homes – but this was a different chapter by itself. For those, the trip went a little further, and that was the concentration camp D a c h a u; probably because the person had refused to do a job that he was forced to do, or that he had not completed the work to the satisfaction of his "supervisors" or was u n a b l e to do so, or perhaps because he uttered a word that had slipped from his tongue in utter embitterment. In such cases, it was wise to do a job without uttering a word and with a countenance that did not reveal anything even if the job was as dirty or as nasty as can be. You had to endure beatings silently, almost thankfully, every whim of these vagabonds you had to follow, whatever kind, otherwise the only other destination was: "C o n c e n t r a t I o n C a m p"

This idea alone made you keep your cool for all misdeeds inflicted on you. Every Jew, also Half-Jew or One-Quarter Jew, that were those of them who had a Jewish wife or vice versa or whose parents or grandparents were of Jewish descent had to suffer from the terror of this gang. Unfortunately, I also was one of the great sufferers of these devilish and ugly treatments. But I must thank God that fate came like it did and not what happened to 10,000's of others who were arrested and transported to a concentration camp. "By one hair" it almost happened to me if I had not suddenly skipped from Vienna. I will get back to that later on.

My brother and I had a clothing shop. The clothes were made by us. We employed a total of about 50 people. 20 of them were employed in our own workshop that was located separately from the storage and showroom. The remaining 30 employees were tailors who picked up work from us and finished it in their homes. It was about these people who had been working for us for almost 3 years to their and our fullest satisfaction, concerning payment and demeanor. But as soon as the political situation had changed, the sudden change in atmosphere had also changed them into hyenas like all others. Hardly 8 days had gone by after the so-called seizure of power, when a tailor by the name of W. came to us suddenly and unexpectedly with a group of S. S. men (Schutz-Staffel)[6], and the Bezirkswalter of the S. A. (Sturmabteilung) Storm Troopers and demanded retroactive payment of wages for the last 2 years because of alleged underpayment of the National Collective Agreement tariffs (it should be mentioned here that we, in Vienna, in our type of business, had a Collective Agreement for tariffs that no manufacturer observed because the tariffs were almost as high as the amounts for which the final clothing was sold.)

The District Administrator asked us where the cash register is. We said that we do not have a cash register and have no money. A thorough search followed by 6 men and they demolished a lot of things, they broke several objects, ripped apart the bedding, cut open feather and cloth ends suspecting hiding places for monies or jewelry, et. etc. and after less than an hour they found our hiding place where our personal effects were hidden. This included 5,400 Marks in cash and a bank savings book for 30,000 Marks. This was for a small private bank that had still been unaffected by these vandals; because at public banks as well as the national Postsparkasse [Bank], right from the first day, all the accounts were blocked – where we also had 14,000 Marks. So, these people left with this loot without leaving a receipt for the monies taken. From now on, every day went by with more agitation and anxiety. The next day, a 2nd group from the S.A. appeared and said that our

---

6 S. S. men (Schutz-Staffel) = paramilitary and security organization of the NSDAP - Bezirkswalter [probably Bezirksverwalter] = District Administrator] - S.A. Sturmabteilung = Storm Troopers or "Brown Shirts," they were the Nazi party's main instrument for undermining democracy and facilitating Adolf Hitler's rise to power.

car was found on the street still in our possession, although from the very first day on, all cars that were kept in garages, were seized. Since we had not put our car in the garage for the last 10 days because we wanted to prevent it from being confiscated, we had stationed it on a different street unattended. This was now interpreted as "concealment of existing assets", we were threatened with a fine and, of course, the car was confiscated right away – never to be seen again. These people even ripped the key of the car out of my brother's hand and took off.

During these 24 hours also a mediation agreement was reached with the tailor who had demanded a payment in arears. He got 1,000 Marks immediately and another 1,000 Marks was awarded to him for the following week. He was content with this amount of money ---- but only in pretense.

He now started to continue the work he began by telling all the other tailors and piece-work foremen about his claim and the success of his demand, also told them about the raid and how much hidden money had been found. This got everyone turned against us and he told them that we would probably pay all claims against us out of fear, etc. This ended in the fact that 3 of our tailors took over our business and workshop; of course, everything happened with the permission of the District Manager of that time who managed the whole matter. Now a Cooperative was formed among the workers who started to manage the business according to their own idea, a so-called N. S. B. Z. G. National Socialist Commercial Cell Association. 5 workers were selected for that – it became apparent that they were the most radical men that were already illegally active in the Nazi Socialist Party during the Schuschnigg regime. These people were not interested in a certain position nor were they driven to accomplish something, but to pull out as much money as possible from the business and as fast as possible as it was possible that in another month, a different manager would come along to take his position; and by then, perhaps, he had not done enough for himself.

In this manner, our business was almost ruined in a short period of time. I said 'almost' because had not Head of a Nazi District, Gauleiter[7] B u e r c k e l, been ordered to Vienna in order to create order, these people would have changed the art and business city Vienna into a dull and bleak city. His own people respected him and so they feared, in advance, for their own fate. Therefore, also the Group Leader in our district who instigated the whole thing at our place, was unlucky and he, himself, ended up in a concentration camp for his misdeeds. But this was only a little piece of justice that was executed and our suffering was not lessened in the least. Daily, men in uniform of the S. A. and S. S. carried away whatever they could and however far it was possible.

So, I constantly lived in fear as to whatever the next day would bring and I did not know whether or not my life was threatened the next day.

Not a day went by that news would not circulate that the S.A. people were wandering around pulling Jews from their homes. As much as possible I always hid from these barbarians who had no human feelings any more inside of them.

There was no sight any longer of the "Vienna heart" they were like beasts, even worse; a beast when full with food and drink becomes milder but these people knew no stopping and did not seem to know where humanity actually began to stop.

The devil got into them and all the hate and anger that they had carried around in their hearts now broke out, like a volcano lets its lava masses stream out, that's how they let their hate and bloodlust stream out to their fellow human beings, the J e w s. No one was exempted.

Picked up off the street I had to go with a horde of these people, clean their clothes, wash cars, clean windows, et. etc.

This compulsory labor by itself did not hurt anyone and no one would have to be afraid of it or would have to hide because of it if you

7 Gauleiter - Head of a Nazi District

were not mistreated at the same time. Anyone who had to carry out this forced labor and behaved calmly and did not make a big scene about it, got a chance and permission to return home after 3 – 4 hours unless, at the next street corner, he was picked up again for the same purpose and any talking back, saying that you just got back from the same type of work, was useless. If, during such an encounter you refused or murmured a word to yourself, you would not see your home again for a while and maybe never again

The worst happening for me took place one day, it was the 7th of May, 1938, when my brother and I were picked up in front of our business by a group of S. S. people. There were 5 people in one of the cars of which hundreds had been stolen. One S. S. man stayed behind, down by the gate to the house, since we had our business on the first floor as already mentioned. Another S.S. man remained in front of the door to the business and 3 men came in clomping loudly with their boots.

It goes without saying, there was no greeting, they had wildly distorted faces, like it always was in such cases. My brother was not at the shop at that time. Only I was there with one of our employees. It was a coincidence that 5 minutes after the invasion of these people into our shop, my brother called by phone to find out if there were any news, but he did not get through to me because one of the S. S. men – when he heard the phone ring – immediately grabbed the receiver as he had taken up his position close to the telephone. After a very short talk during which he found out that my brother was on the other side of the line, he demanded that my brother came to the shop immediately if he wanted to prevent that an order for his arrest was going to be issued. After this threat, no more than 10 minutes went by and by this time, my brother and I sat in the car and rode with these 5 men for almost ½ hour out and around the city without actually knowing what they wanted to do with the two of us. All this happened at such speed that we had no time to inform our wives, and the shop stayed in the hands of one of our employees. Finally, after ½ hour's drive, we got to a neighborhood of villas in Döbling, as I recognized the area right away. This belonged to the 19th community district of Vienna, an area where the richest people of Vienna had lived. I did, however, no recognize the street and the house; later on I saw the address: "Lannerstrasse 36".

It was a great, magnificent villa that had belonged to a very rich Jew. The villa was converted into a casern, a casino and drink hole for the S. S. people, a group of about 40 people.

They sat in the easy chairs that were there, put their feet up on the table, some played billiards, drank wine and liqueurs, probably the basement is filled with alcohol racks, others played around with their weapons – in short, they did everything they could not to get bored.

They greeted us forcefully – I still remember it clearly until today. Right at the interior after passing the entrance door two lines of S. S. men were standing who greeted us. My brother and I had to pass by this line and we were kicked by each of these barbarians with their heavy, black boots so that we ended up in the corner of the room. Later they told us to take off our coats and led us down to their basement.

While going down, we already heard loud screams of two men. The screams shook us to the core. Once down there, we were ordered to clean and tidy up the basement as if it were a living room. This was no easy task, as you can imagine, straw, coal, iron, diverse equipment, potatoes and other junk had to be put in order and the other rooms, a total of 4, had to be cleaned to the utmost. The floor of these basement rooms were probably never properly cleaned since the house was built, the coal dust seemed to be grown into the floor and we were forced to scratch it out with our fingernails, since no soap or brushes were given to us. Each time the rag had to be cleaned or rinsed off, we had to get fresh water from the courtyard and that was our luck; this interval was always our rest and relaxation, even if some of their buddies wanted to brag to the others and used us as practice goals for their weapons and shot close to us to scare us; but we probably would have collapsed due to lack of strength if we would not have been able to make those trips to the courtyard.

These jobs were always carried out under supervision of an S. S. man who always carried a stick in his hand in case he had to chastise us, perhaps for not working fast enough or, perhaps, he just felt like it. Sometimes he left his supervisory post and went up to the upper level for some time since he was craving some Schnapps like his other buddies who were already in the process of getting seriously drunk. Once, I used this opportunity to rest a little and to look around to see where this screaming was coming from which we heard continuously.

Then I saw in another room – which I also had to get to know later on – the scene of horror. A man in his 40's, probably a physician by profession, since he wore a white coat as was the custom with physicians, lay on the floor and above him knelt an S. S. man who also carried a stick and he beat on the physician continuously with these words:

"DIRTY JEW; JEWISH PIG shout out with loud voice that you are a Jew." This physician, however, seemed to be obstinate, and shouted with a hoarse voice, since he had been mistreated for quite a while:

"I a m a G e r m a n"

He had barely finished his exclamation and the cane beatings came down on him again like hailstones. When I saw this, my blood started boiling like in an oven – I wanted to jump over there and help the man, but at the last moment, it became clear to me that it would surely mean my death, since I am a prisoner here also.

Therefore, I had to return to my workplace, fearing that this could still happen to us, my brother and me.

During my short way back, passing a closed door, I saw, peeking through the keyhole, a well-dressed lady who tried to wash mountains of dishes like plates, bowls, glasses, etc. that had come down from the "gentlemen's" feasting. I could see from the work that was in front of her that she could not manage that – shortly before we left the house, she collapsed.

I had not been back from my exploratory walk to my workplace for more than a second when our guard came down the stairs.

Finally, after 5 hours of work, everything had been put in best order and we believed that we could go home now. Sweat ran down our foreheads and our bodies steamed under our shirts as if we were horses. But we were very much in error if we thought we would be free to go home already. The guard led us to the temporary commandant who inquired as to whether we had done our work well and proper. When the guard confirmed this, the commandant now ordered us to put our jackets back on and we let our faces gain brightness again, because we were happy – just nodded to each other and communicating with our eyes, since we had assumed partially because of our good conduct and partially because of our work that was done well, that they would have mercy with us. But our assumption was very wrong.

Each of us was given a bucket full of flour paste and a brush and for each of us 2 S. S. men as guards. They were men in black uniform who carried large placards that we now had to paste to street walls and planks. That's how we went through 3 districts of Vienna, through Döbling, Grinzing, and Sievering. From wall to wall, from plank to plank. This propaganda effort announced the newest edition of the periodical: "D a s s c h w a r z e K o r p s" ["T h e B l a c k Co r p s"] that appeared 8 days later with a special edition, clearly with the ugliest J e w - b a i t i n g.

Wherever we went to paste these notifications, a crowd gathered, people came together, be it curiosity seekers or hell-raisers who wanted to show their "high education" by spitting in our faces and with loud laughter and their goofy screaming acted crazily with joy; in their thoughts rejoicing about what excellent deed they had just accomplished; it was a shame to have to admit:

T h e s e people are also Austrians. In many cases, there were also people in the group who were ashamed of such behavior and distanced themselves from the others because they could not witness such horrible deeds and would have liked to say something in response if they, themselves, did not have to fear to be beaten up.

Since our accompaniment, our 2 S. S. guards had not taken too many of the placards with them, thank God we were already done by 5:30 p.m. and following a steady march we got back at exactly 6:00 p.m. at the villa of the S.S. company.

Our feet had hardly touched the basement floor when I saw suddenly that the color of my brother's face had suddenly changed. He looked extremely pale and seemed about to collapse. I first thought this was weakness from the difficult work and having been frightened or from hunger – but the sight of the high commander just entering from another door told me that something else must be the case. He also had suddenly changed the color in his face, but not to white or pale but to fire-red; probably because of anger; but his face was red like a crab. So I thought right away, now there is going to be a thunder storm and I was right!

Again we were led down to the basement but to the place where they had beaten the physician so badly. We suddenly felt cold. I don't know whether it was from fear or from the stone floor of the basement or whether it was the eeriness of the room.

Right away we were surrounded by about 10 S.S. people and one of them ordered us to "stand at attention" in expectation of the arrival of the commandant. Shortly after that, he came, indeed, running down the steps and went straight ahead to my brother with the words:

"Dirty Jewish Pig, do you remember me?" My brother answered: "No, Sir". As soon as he had said that, he got a slap in the face from behind, where the other S. S. men stood and at such force that I thought his face must be out of steel since no blood spritzed from his skin. And again the order came: "Stand at attention", and the commandant went on: "You dirty Jew, I will help you out, remembering." "Recall, it was about 4 years ago when you worked at the D. K. company in the N. street as manipulator and I had a disagreement with the boss about various wage shortcomings and you kicked me out of the shop, is that right, you damned Jewish Pig?" My brother replied: "No, Sir, you are mistaken, that must have been another person." And again he was slapped in the face from behind as before. Finally, he could see that any denial in such a case would really only harm him and, therefore affirmed any further question. I stood there with clenched fists and fast heart beats and I am still surprised at this time that I was able to keep my cool and calm nerves and did not react untamed. After this incident, the commandant continued:

"I know that you have your own business today and your piece-workers also had some wage claims from you – when, Jew, are you thinking about paying that? My brother had no time to think about that for a long time, because the slaps and beatings by stick came down on him again and I, also got some of them. And he said: "In 3 – 4 days I will have everything settled with my workers". (It should be noted that the claims by our workers were totally illegal and the majority of the workers did not even want to approach us but they were forced by the newly founded N. S. B. Z. G.) = [approx.] National socialist Commercial Cell Association "No, you nasty Jew", were the next words by the S. S. leader, "Tomorrow evening at 6:00 o'clock both of you will be back here with the receipts of your workers, indicating that everything was paid to the last penny. Otherwise I will show up at your place at 7:00 o'clock with my people and then . . .. you will feel a lot better."

We agreed quickly to everything in order to get out of this hell still alive.

Finally, they searched all of our pockets and whatever monies were found, were confiscated with the explanation that this was for the gasoline used for the trip to this place. The pocket search did not materialize in more than 9 Marks.

Now we were finally on the street and we walked as fast as we could, as it was always possible that one of the men thought of something for which they could use us.

After a 2 ½-hour march, we finally got home, tired and exhausted with the strong resolution to flee from this purgatory and leave everything behind.

That's what really happened then. For me, fleeing was a difficult and dangerous matter, since besides my wife, I also have a child for whose safety I had to care. But finally I did not seem to have any other choice as such a precarious flight across the borders since all doors that I had tried that were legal were shut for me.

Surprisingly enough, 2 days later I already received my passport which I had applied and asked for a month before that time. But the passport alone was not enough to leave, you also had to have additional papers from governmental agencies, such as Tax certificate, customs papers and a certificate of Good Conduct, etc. etc. And finally, you had to have a visa for a foreign country – that was the most important thing – and that was exactly that which was not available.

Now we spoke about our escape. We chose May 12, 1938, at 9 o'clock at night. I was supposed to flee as second person on May 13, 1938 with the aid of the same two men who were to help my brother and sister-in-law escape across the border.

Since the flight occurred during the night and was dangerous, because the escape was to go via a small lake with a tiny little canoe, there was no possibility for any of us to have more than 1 small suitcase with the most necessary things; especially a second suit, since, most likely, we would have to wade through a part of swamp or marsh.

According to our plan, my brother was to inform me of the successful crossing immediately by telegram with contents: Congratulations on your birthday. This covert telegram was to arrive at my house at the latest by 9:00 in the morning. If the crossing did not go well, there was to be no message.

As "friendship reward" he left my house, heavily loaded with monies and goods.

At 4:00 o'clock in the afternoon, suddenly 2 men came from the Gestapo to me to the shop and asked for my brother. I told him I did not know where he was at that time. In my opinion he was with a customer in Steiermark and will return after a few days. Then, they continued: "We have learned that you want to emigrate, is that true?" and I answered: "Yes, as soon as I receive the permission from the government and also have the necessary papers. Then I am inclined to emigrate and I am also forced to do so, since the present government orders me to leave just like many other 100,000 of Jews who just like I, were even born in Vienna."

"Where is your passport that we have issued to you a little while ago." One of them asked.

"My wife has that passport with her", I said, "since she is taking care of this matter because I have no time for it."

"Good" said the officials "we will come back tonight at 7:00 o'clock; would you prepare all the documents for us in the meantime, including the passport."

Now I knew that no time was to be lost. Immediately, at home I gave orders to pack a few of our things. There were 2 small suitcases, since we are taking the next train to C. S. R. [Czech Republic].

Quickly, I still gathered our business journals and customer registers and brought them away and locked up the shop as well as the workshop and at the next occasion, threw the keys away where they could not ever be found again. Everything stayed in its place as before. The only thing that I took along, that is, that I gave for safekeeping to my driver for my further use were my two material cutting machines. Having returned home from this hasty errand, I stayed in the same suit that I wore that day, packed the 2 suitcases that were already sitting there and off we went to the railroad station – without any Good-Bye to my mother or my siblings. Before the train took off, I telephoned my sister and told her about my leaving and asked her to please speak to my mother and ask her forgiveness that I took off like that without speaking a word with her.

I could hardly wait for the train to take off, my wife and I were so nervous and excited and thought if I would only be on the other side of the Austrian border already.

I had in mind that there might still come some difficulties and, indeed, I was not lucky enough to cross the border easily and today, I must really say – knowing all the incidents that were to happen – that I had God with me as my protector.

We had hardly reached the Czech border when a German official in civil clothing came into our compartment and asked me, whether I did not have a brother and what his first name was? At this moment I saw everything lightning fast fly by me and everything was clear to me and I also comprehended our situation.

Namely, that my brother and his wife were caught here when they tried to illegally cross the border and were incarcerated and that the authorities could, therefore, be exactly informed. That's why it now meant to keep steady and not to reveal oneself or by any unwise action get my brother into trouble; it was already considered a crime if anyone tried to cross the border without permission or without consideration of all regulations, like my brother had done. "Where are you traveling to"? then asked the official. I am traveling to the spa resort Pystian for treatment which you can also see from my visa – I suffer from rheumatic pain and since I never travel far or near without my wife and child, therefore I have also taken them along today."

"Do you suffer from the same illness as your brother? That is quite peculiar. You do not look sick at all", he went on to say. So I replied that after all we are one family and have the same parents; so an illness like this could surely affect all siblings. Now I saw that the official became perplexed and baffled as he had probably not expected such a fitting answer because he probably thought that he could embarrass me perhaps and guide me into a trap. In spite of that, I was now forced to go down to a revision station with all the luggage and my wife and child. I have to specially stress here that I was the only traveler in my compartment – and in the whole train there were probably no more than 10 travelers who, at this time, especially from Vienna, had already been able to gather all the necessary documents and papers in order to be able to emigrate orderly and legally.

In those days, in May of 1938, there were still difficulties and obstacles to overcome, for businessmen almost unattainable.

In the revision hall, there were 6 border officials from the German and 4 from the Czech side.

My wife and the child were immediately taken for questioning and for examination in another room.

First the search began for jewelry, expensive things, things that were not allowed to be exported, monies, etc. etc. Everything not nailed down tightly was ripped open and cut open, my camera was taken apart, soles were ripped from shoes, at the suitcase straps, the seams were split open and the lining in my suit was completely undone; thank God I only had 3 suits with me of which I wore one, otherwise this examination would have taken until the next morning if I had another 3 or 4 of them. By coincidence, one breast area of a suit felt a little stiffer than usual and the people became suspicious and thought they had caught me, perhaps just like with my brother who had had the nerve to take along a little more money than was actually allowed – for them, the object was to find something illegal in order to send someone to the concentration camp. After the lining had now been cut out entirely, it was discovered that the interlining material was a little harder than was usual when suits were initially sewn. All officials were very surprised about that, of course I mean those from the German side, and asked me then with a laughing tone why this is the case and they wanted me to explain to them how this was done since I was from this line of work. In spite of my fears and sufferings I still had to give them a little instructional explanation about this procedure so that the officials could understand it better. In the meantime, they examined my wife and child thoroughly in the other room. Not one body part was left untouched. When the officials were finally done with their so-called customs revision, of course our train was no longer in the station. It had left almost ½ hour ago and was at full speed by now.

It was already 10:30 at night. My child lay on a bench and slept, protected by a Czech woman who had just visited her husband, a border employee who was at work at that time. All in all, the Czech officials were quite impatient and annoyed about the harassment and bad treatment of us by the German border organization and they tried several times to get our passports that were in the hands of the Gestapo, with the remarks that our passports and other paperwork was in order and our thorough bodily examination had not yielded anything illegal either. But this man did not let the passport out of his hands and said to me: "You must stay here and remain over night as I have to wait until tomorrow morning to find out more things about you from Vienna or if you are willing to pay for a long-distance call to Vienna, then I will do that now." I replied that he knew very well that I only have 15 Marks since this was the maximum legal limit and that I would really need this small amount of money for the immediate future.

But since I am forced to spend tonight at this town which, of course, also costs money, I would rather risk spending the amount necessary for the long-distance call to Vienna in order to avoid having to spend the night here.

Shortly after that he came back and said that he could not get any connection by phone to Vienna and that I must really go and find quarters here for the night.

(Incidental Remark:) (Several months later, I found out from my brother who had been incarcerated for 4 months because of crossing the borders illegally, that during this critical time when our examination happened at the borders, that is, we were also trapped at the German gendarmerie station just like he and that this Gestapo man had not actually called Vienna but only came down to me to find out more information and conduct an investigation which, however, was just as unsuccessful. My brother found out that this man was supposed to call Vienna by overhearing the conversation with that man's colleagues.)

Led by a Czech railway man – I had my sleeping son in my arms – we wandered through the town searching. Altogether there were 4 guesthouses in the town and they were all overcrowded, nowhere was there a bed for the night. The reason for this was that at this border, a lot of Czech military was stationed and, therefore, all guesthouses, hotels and private pensions were overcrowded.

We then returned to the border station without having found any quarters and we lay down on a bench for the night.

Meanwhile, I saw that one of the higher border employees and a Gestapo man got into a heated argument that ended with the fact that the Czechs ended up in possession of my passport and promptly, actually at the speed of lightening, impressed their stamps in it. This was not even one second too early, as the stationmaster was about to give the starting signal for the train that had already been waiting there. This was at 1:45 in the morning and it was the last train for the day.

We quickly jumped from the bench, each of us grabbed a suitcase, thanked the Czech officials and for the next ½ hour we were unable to speak because of fear, joy, surprise and heart-pounding, although the train had long since traveled through Czech lands.

My father could never bring himself to write more or to revisit these memories.....

Of a full life –

Profound learning experiences have come from my fortunate interaction with so many people, of different backgrounds, in so many different countries.

I met thousands professionally, socially, over long periods of time and had wonderful discussions, professional relations, and social interactions.

People are all very much the same and have left me with one deep impression:

We are masters of our actions until we speak or act, but once we do, our deeds and words live on, master us and are irrevocable

Andy & Erin   Harry & Rhea   Ross & Robin Abby & Darryl Debra & Scott Sarah Melissa& Alex

ABOUT THE AUTHOR

Dr. Harry Rein, the first doctor, lawyer, and judge to practice all three professions at the same time, escaped from the Nazis, was a refugee for many years, and with good fortune landed in the United States.

Rein was one of the first Board Certified family practitioners in Florida in 1960. He practiced for twenty years, then became a medical malpractice lawyer, reviewing over 15,000 events and participating in over three hundred trials. His involvement in such cases was controversial in the 1970s, newsworthy in the 1980s, and has since gone on to be used as teaching guides.

After being sworn into the Supreme Court of the United States, he was enlisted into the Inns of Court and started the Inns of Court in the Orlando, Central Florida area. Rein was later appointed as a part-time judge with the Nuclear Regulatory Commission and selected to attend the Army War College.

Glossary

As a very brief summary of the fruitful life Rhea and I have led, here is a summary of places we visited, and those where I have worked and consulted.

Countries visited

Algeria, Antigua, Argentina, Aruba, Australia, Austria, Bahamas, Barbados, Belarus, Bora Bora, Bosnia and Herzegovina, Botswana, Bulgaria, Cambodia, Canada, Chile, China, Colombia, Costa Rica, Croatia, Cuba, Czech Republic, Denmark, Ecuador, Egypt, Estonia, Falkland Islands, Fiji, Finland, France, French Polynesia, Germany, Gibraltar, Great Britain, Greece, Greenland, Grenada, Hong Kong, Hungary, Iceland, Indonesia, Ireland, Israel, Italy, Jamaica Japan, Jordan, Latvia, Lithuania, Luxembourg, Malaysia, Maldives, Mali, Malta, Martinique, Mexico, Monaco, Morocco, Myanmar, Nassau, Netherlands, New Caledonia, New Zealand, Nicaragua, Norway, Palestinian territories, Panama, Peru, Portugal, Puerto Rico, Romania, Russian Federation, Saint Kitts and Nevis, Saint Lucia, Scotland, Serbia, Singapore, Slovakia, (Slovak Republic) Slovenia, South Africa, Spain, St Vincent's, Sweden, Switzerland, Syria, Tahiti, Taiwan, Thailand, Tibet, Tonga, Tunisia, Turkey, Ukraine, Uruguay, Vatican City, Vietnam, Virgin Islands (British), Virgin Islands (U.S.), Zambia, Zimbabwe.

Medical Legal consultations

Austria, Canada, China, Egypt, France, Germany, Mexico, Russia, South Africa, Tibet, Zimbabwe

The Professional Life of
Harry Rein, J.D. M.D.

General Activities

Dr. Harry Rein is the only active physician, trial lawyer and retired judge in the U.S.

Dr. Rein practices pro hac vice in multiple jurisdictions and has been invited to give legal advice and discuss U.S. policy on every Continent except the "ice" ones.

He is a teacher, author and known speaker.

Practiced general medicine, surgery and obstetrics, 1957 - 1980.

U.S. Army Medical Corps, Captain 1957-1960.

Currently a trial lawyer concentrating on medical malpractice cases.

Judge with the Nuclear Regulatory Commission, 1990 to 2003.

Civilian invitee at U.S. Army War College on strategy - 2007

Financial Planning and Advisor for Professionals

Registered arbitrator with FINRA

Admitted to Practice in the United States Supreme Court.

American Inns of Court -- Founder and Charter Member, First Central Florida Inn.

Developer of the "Damage Control Through Zero Defects" system.© 1987

A unique medical malpractice prevention program.

Results include $5.1 million dollar jury verdict and other multi-million dollar verdicts and settlements.

Academic Experiences

New York University Undergraduate School, 1953.

State University of N.Y. Downstate Medical Center, M.D. 1957

University of Florida, College of Law, J.D. 1982

University of Florida, College of Medicine, Preceptor.

University of Florida, Clinical Professor of Medicine.

Florida Hospital Internship Program, Instructor.

University of Florida, School of Nursing - Curriculum written.

Nova University College of Law - Hospital Risk Management Program.

Postgraduate Teaching Faculty - Canadian Memorial Chiropractic College.

Owner - Medical School for Attorneys© & Law School for Doctors© courses.

Faculty - Dep't of Medical Education, UCF College of Medicine.

Consultation Assignments

Agency for Health Care Administration, State of Florida - Advisor, 1993.

U.S. Army -- Evaluation of Disability Claims, 1958 - 1960.

Orange County, Florida, Assistant Medical Examiner, 1960 - 1964.

Orange County, Florida, Consultant to County Judge, 1960 - 1968.

U.S. Selective Service System -- Consultant.

Florida Department of Vocational Rehabilitation -- Consultant.

Department of Professional Regulation, State of Florida -- Consultant.

Dr Harry Rein JD MD

Professional Associations

American Academy of Family Physicians -- Fellow.
American Academy of Thermography -- Diplomate.
American Bar Association.
American Board of Clinical Thermology -- Diplomate.
American Board of Family Practice -- Diplomate.
American College of Legal Medicine -- Fellow.
American Herschel Society.
American Medical Association.
American Pain Society.
Association of Trial Lawyers of America.

Florida Academy of Family Physicians.
Florida Bar.
Florida Medical Association.
Florida Trial Lawyers Association.
International Thermographic Society.
Orange County Medical Society.
Southern Medical Association.
Multiple Physician Recognition Awards.**
Distinguished service awards: Pres. Johnson & Nixon for efforts to the U.S. government.

Medical and Law Seminars, Audio and Video Series Prepared and Presented by Harry Rein, J.D. M.D.

- Approved medical malpractice, Risk Management and Money Management seminars.
- Medical Malpractice Litigation Courses sponsored by various organization over years.
- Trial Technique and Discovery seminars approved for required continuing credits.
- Courses were approved for CME & CLE credits by Medical

Associations and State Bar Associations.

Academy of Florida Trial Lawyers. *
Advanced Advocacy College, A.T.L.A. *
AFTL - Soft Tissue Injuries. *
AIDS in Florida.
Akron City General Hospital.
Alaska Thermography.
American Association of Gynecologic Laparoscopists. *
American College of Legal Medicine.
American Pain Society.
Arkansas Bar Association.
Arkansas Trial Lawyers Association. *
Association of Trial Lawyers of America. *
Atlanta Bar Association.

Australia Medico-Legal Thermography (Sydney).
Auto Torts Seminars. *
Beaumont Hospitals.
Belli Seminars. *
Canadian Memorial Chiropractic College
Central Florida Claims Association.
C.M.E. Co. of Acadiana, LA.
Computer Management, Orlando.
Current Concepts Seminars. *
Dryden Co. -- Surplus Insurance.
Federal Rules of Evidence. *
Florida Academy of Family Practice.
Florida Claims Association.

Florida Shorthand Reporters Association.

Flu Vaccine Seminar -- Washington, D.C.

Gynecological Endoscopic Workshop, Zimbabwe.

Gynecologic Endoscopy for Residents, Dallas TX.

Hampton Seminars. *

International Conference on Legal Medicine.

International Conference on Thermal Assessment.

International Conferences (on Medical Malpractice).

International Educational Seminars. *

International Medical Centers HMO & Hospital Malpractice Risk Management.

Indiana Trial Lawyers Association.

International Educ. Seminars - Medical Malpractice. *

International Thermography Society. *

Jacksonville Bar Association.

Kentucky Trial Lawyers Association. *

Laparoscopic Litigation Group - ATLA.

Litigation Techniques in the 80's.

Louisiana Trial Lawyers Association. *

Massachusetts Academy of Trial Attorneys.

Medical School for Lawyers in 2 days. *

Medi-Legal Institute - for doctors and risk managers.

Medi-Legal Institute - for lawyers.

Medi-Legal Seminars - for risk managers.

Michigan Trial Lawyers Association.

Mississippi Claims Association. *

Missouri Trial Lawyers Association.

National Practice Institute Seminars. *

Nationwide Insurance Company.

New Jersey Chiropractic Society.

North Dakota Law School.

Nova University Law Center.

Ochsner Foundation - New
Approaches-Antimicrobials
Okaloosa-Walton Bar
Association.
Oklahoma Bar Association - 2
d. Tort program
Qmax Medical Training.
Oregon Board of Chiropractic
Examiners.
Outpatient Ophthalmic
Surgical Society - 1988.
Orlando Claims Association.
Palm Beach Claims
Association.
Palm Beach Regional
Hospital.
Palmer College of
Chiropractic.
Parker College.
Pediatric Oncology Group --
Gainesville, Florida.
Pensacola Legal Assistants.
Personal Injury Seminars -
1980,–1984 (FL). *
Princess Cruise Lines -
(programs aboard ship)*
Progressive Insurance
Company.
Prudential Property and
Casualty. *

Queen Elizabeth II
Seminars
Risk Management
Consultants.
Rollins College.
San Diego Surgical Society
Second World Cong.
of Endoscopic Female
Sterilization.
Seminole Comm. College -
"The People's Law School"
Society of Laparoendoscopic
Surgeons. *
South Carolina Trial Lawyers
Association. *
Southern Medical Association
* -- 1984.
    Medical Malpractice
Lectures to Sections on:
    Neurology, Neurosurg.,
Psychiatry, Radiology.
Southern Medical Association
- 1985.
    Medical Malpractice
Lectures to Sections on:
        Anesthesiology, Chest
        Diseases, Family
        Practice, Colon
        & Rectal Surgery,
        Medicine, Surgery,

Urology, Pediatrics &
Adolescent Medicine,
and Plastic & Recon.
Surgery.
Southern Medical Association
- 1992.
  Medical Malpractice
Lectures to the Sections on:
  Chest Diseases,
  Orthopedic &
  Traumatic Surgery,
  Colon and Rectal
  Surgery, Emergency
  Medicine, Medicine,
  Obstetrics,
  Neurology &
  Psychiatry, Urology,
  Ophthalmology,
  and Plastic &
  Reconstructive
  Surgery.
Stetson University.
Surplus and Excess Lines
Claims Association.
Tampa Claims Managers
Council.

Tennessee Trial Lawyers
Association. *
Travcon (Travel the
Continents). *
University of Alabama.
University of Capetown, Sth.
Africa, Gyn Endoscopics
University of Florida College
of Law.
University of Missouri
- Columbia.
University of South Carolina
Law School.
Various Insurance Companies. *
Various Medical Groups. *
Volusia County Bar
Association. *
Volusia County Medical
Society.
Waterman Hospital - Risk
Management.
West Boca Raton Medical
Center.
  Risk Management and
Damage Control.

* Repeated visits and presentations

Publications

Medical School for Attorneys course - Approved for CLE & Ethics credit in Fl., La., Ar., Ga.
Weight of Medical Evidence CD lecture series - - Florida Bar approved CLE credit

Medical School for Attorneys – DVD 16 hr series 2006, 2007
Weight of Medical Evidence – 12 hr CD lecture series 2006, 2007
Law School for Doctors (text) - 2002
Legal System & Art of Medicine - Laparoscopy 2002
The ATLA (Ark.) Trial Docket – Malpractice Discovery
Current Opinions in Obs/Gyn - Complications.... - Lippincott
Management of Laparoscopic Surgical Complications – text chapter
Put Some Order in Your Life.
Exclusive Contracts.
Injuries and Litigation in Gyn Endoscopy & Laparoscopy
Unveiling Laparoscopic Malpractice
Unraveling the Mysteries of Medical Malpractice.
Managed Care and Medical Malpractice.
Damage Control Through Zero Defects.
The Primer on Medical Malpractice -- textbook.
The Weight of Medical Evidence -- text and cassette lecture series.
Thermographic Evidence of Soft Tissue Injuries -- textbook.
    Shepard's McGraw - Hill 1987. Supplemented annually 1988 - 1992.
The Primer on Thermography -- textbook.
The Primer on Soft Tissue Injuries -- textbook.

The Primer on Soft Tissue Injuries -- Revisited and Revised 1993
Legal Medicine 1986 (Thermography)
Medical Malpractice, A Thoughtbook -- textbook, 1992, 1996.
Medi-Legal Ch. in: Management of Laparoscopic Surgical
Complications- 2004
Newspapers Columns and Commentator:
    Ocular Surgery News Orthopedics Today
    Radiology Today. Japan - Sun Contact Lens News Letter.
    Ophthalmology Management.
Quality Review Bulletin of JCAH -- Commentary: It Happens
on Weekends.
Southern Medical Journal -- multiple abstracts.
Legal Aspects of Medical Practice, ACLM -- Thermography.
Medical Malpractice Prevention -- Medical Malpractice Update.
American Chiropractor -- Thermography, Medical-Legal
Implications.
Belli Law Journal -- Proving Soft Tissue Injuries in Court -
Thermography.
Physician Negligence -- Guidelines for Attorneys.
Trial -- Thermography: Medical and Legal Implications.
Florida Chiropractic Association Journal -- Thermographic
Applications.
American Chiropractor -- Chiropractic in the Courtroom.
The Medical Expert.
Medical Evidence -- The Physician's Viewpoint.
The Horizontal Review of Medical Records.
Evaluating the Personal Injury Claim.
The Medical Injury Dollar.
Medicine's Bermuda Triangle.
Antibodies as Antihormones.
Metabolism: Excretion of Sodium Load Pre-eclampsia.

Radio and TV Talk Shows Co-Hosted or Guest

Dr. Rein has guested and hosted radio and TV talk shows and his own **TV MEDICAL ACTION LINE**. Appearances:

AB-TV	New Orleans
BLAB-TV	Pensacola
CABLE-A	Orlando
CABLE-TV	US
CABLE-W	St Pete.
KFTP	Minneapolis
KING	Seattle
KIRO	Seattle
KLIF	Dallas
KMOX	St Louis
KRLD	Dallas
STORER-TV	Louisville
WABC	New York
WAVE	Louisville
WAVE-TV	Louisville
WDBO	Orlando
WCPX-TV	Orlando
WERD	Bradenton
WESH-TV	Orlando
WFPL	Louisville
WFTL-TV	Orlando
Independent Broadcasters Network	
WFTS-TV	Tampa
WGY	Schenectady
WIOD	Miami
WISN	Milwaukee

WJJD	Chicago
WJNO	W. PalmBch.
WJR	Detroit
WKIS	Orlando
WLAC	Nashville
WMAQ	Chicago
WMFE-TV	Orlando
WOAI	San Antonio
WOFL-TV	Orlando
WPBR	Palm Beach
WPTV-TV	W. PalmBch.
WSN-TV	US
WTTB	Vero Beach
WTKN	Seminole
WTKX	Pensacola
WQYK	St. Pete.
WWL	New Orleans

Made in the USA
Lexington, KY
07 March 2016